M000248016

Interactive
Children's
Sermons
52 Messages from
The Psalms

Linda Carlblom

Standard
PUBLISHING
Bringing The Word to Life™

Cincinnati, Ohio

Standard Publishing, Cincinnati, OH. A division of Standex International Corporation.
©2001 by Linda Carlblom. All rights reserved.
Printed in the United States of America.
08   07   06   05   9   8   7   6   5   4   3
ISBN 0-7847-1267-0

All Scripture quotations are taken from the HOLY BIBLE, NEW INTERNATIONAL VERSION®.
NIV®. Copyright © 1973, 1978, 1984 by International Bible Society. Used by permission of
Zondervan Publishing House. All rights reserved.

Edited by Theresa C. Hayes
Cover design by Diana Walters
Inside design by Ewa Pol

Dedication

This book is lovingly dedicated to the

memory of my dear friend, my fifth-

and sixth-grade Sunday school teacher,

Marge McPherson, whose love for me

and devotion to Christ impacted my

life profoundly and eternally.

Contents

∗ No supplies are needed for this message.

Acknowledgements

My thanks go out to my writers critique group, Tuesday's Children, who have helped me learn to write, encouraged me in my dreams, and prayed for me along my journey. My love and appreciation for each of you is beyond words.

To the Lakeshore Bible Church for allowing me to stretch my wings in children's ministry, and to the children there who have listened to countless children's messages. Thank you for your love and encouragement week after week.

To my sister, Marsha, who has been there for me since birth and whom I can't imagine life without. You've been my best friend, my mentor, and my fellow dream chaser.

To my parents, who were, and continue to be, the best teachers I ever had. Your unconditional love and example have given me the confidence to live out my life in Christ boldly.

To my children, Jessica, Tyler, and Ashley. You give me daily doses of joy, smiles, and promise for the future. Thank you for who you are and who you are becoming.

And finally, to Rollin, my husband and encourager. You always said I could do this and never stopped believing in me. Thanks for your constant love and support through this project. You have shared with me my most cherished moments. Lucky me to have you to share my life's journey.

How To Use This Book

Wait!

Before you put this book back on the shelf thinking, "I don't have time to coordinate volunteers and rehearsals," let me assure you, you don't need a surplus of time to use this book. Believe me, I'm no stranger to the feeling of waking up on Sunday morning thinking, "Hmm. I wonder what I'll do for a children's message today." I've spent many rides to church frantically flipping the pages of my Bible looking for something I could apply on a child's level. If you can relate, then this book is for you. Here's why.

The messages are taken from the psalms and present practical ideas to apply to a child's life. The straightforward, easy-to-understand style of the psalms make them natural subject matter for use with children. Many children already relate to David as the boy who killed Goliath and are eager to hear what else he, and the other psalm writers, had to say.

Each message contains some degree of interaction between the children and members of the congregation—sometimes the entire congregation! This interaction helps the adults become more involved in the discipleship of the children, and allows the entire church body, rather than just the Sunday school teachers or pastor, to affirm the children. This method of teaching draws children into the fold of the church family, just as Jesus, the Good Shepherd, draws us unto him.

You may be asking yourself, "But what if our children have their own separate worship service? Will these interactive messages still work without the presence of an entire congregation?" The answer is a resounding "Yes!" These messages are easily adaptable to fit your needs. Here are a few suggestions:

1 Recruit a few members of your congregation to help out for five minutes in your children's service. Most volunteers won't mind missing a few minutes of their own service if they're asked to do so only occasionally. Assure them that they can return to their own worship service when they're finished.

2 Does your church have a drama team? Let them use their talents to assist in children's worship a few minutes each week. High school and college students are also good resources for volunteers.

3 Depending on how your children's worship is structured, you may be able to use some of the older children as volunteers in these messages. Or you can use your entire young audience in place of the adults when the entire congregation participates. The kids will love being able to wiggle and praise God at the same time!

4 Following each message are options for medium and low interaction. The medium interaction will simplify the message, using only one or two volunteers, and the low interaction gives you an idea of how you can present the message on your own if you absolutely don't want to bother recruiting volunteers. At all interaction levels, the majority of the volunteer involvement is so simple individuals can be asked to help ten minutes prior to the worship service—no rehearsals are necessary.

So how do you recruit volunteer help? I've found the most effective way is to give folks the general idea of the message and what their parts will be. Handing someone a script (especially ten minutes before the message) is far too intimidating. The unspoken instruction becomes, "Here's the script. Hope you can memorize it in ten minutes." The pressure is on and you'll be lucky to have a volunteer. If you tell them the general idea of what's going to be said and how they should respond, they're much more comfortable and willing to help. I explain to them that there are no specific lines they need to say. Even the paragraphs that look like a script are to be used only as guidelines. The dialogue is set up this way to make it easy to see who is doing what, but assure your participants that the lines are only suggestions. In this way, the exchange with your volunteers during the message will be more relaxed and sound more natural. Allow your volunteers to have fun, too! Let them ham it up if they want! Their contributions will just add to the joy of the message.

Of course, if you're not a last-minute person, you can always call your potential volunteers during the week and ask for their help. The more time you give them to think about their parts, the more they may surprise you with their creativity! A few of the sermons do, in fact, require a little preparation, such as gathering costumes, or collecting as many trash can lids as you have children.

If you're like me, on some busy Sunday mornings, you may spend more time trying to find a super-simple, no-supplies-needed message than you do actually studying it. While I'm not condoning ill preparedness, I do accept the reality that some weeks it's impossible to be as prepared as you'd like. *Interactive Children's Sermons* solves that problem for you. The table of contents is coded with asterisks (*) next to the messages that require no supplies. It also lists the messages by topic and by Scripture. Use this information to tailor your message to your children's particular needs, a certain season or theme, or your pastor's sermon and Scripture text.

Be creative! Reading through these messages may spark an idea for a different way to present them that would be more suitable to your style and church. Maybe you have a different prop you'd like to use, or a different Scripture to tie in with the sermon. Use this book as a springboard for your imagination.

You never know how far-reaching your impact will be on one young life—maybe even one old life. May you be richly blessed as you leave the imprint of God's love on some of his favorite people—children.

The Hearing Test

THEME: God hears us

SCRIPTURE: "The Lord will hear when I call to him" (Psalm 4:3).

SUPPLIES NEEDED: None

INTERACTION: *Have the congregation yell, whisper, and think the word "help" on cue.*

We're going to give everyone a hearing test today. It's nothing to be worried about because it will be more like a game than a test. Are you ready? On the count of three, I'd like the entire congregation to yell the word "Help!" as loud as you can. Are you ready? One, two, three! (*Congregation yells "Help!"*) Wow! That was pretty loud! Did anyone have any trouble hearing that?

OK, now let's have everyone whisper the same thing. Ready? One, two, three! (*Congregation whispers "Help!"*) How was that, kids? Could you still hear that? (*Let children respond.*) Was it as easy to hear as when they yelled? (*Let children respond.*) Why not? (*Let children respond.*)

How about if we just think the word "Help"? Let's see what that's like. On the count of three, everyone think "Help!" as hard as you can. Ready? One, two, three. (*Pause to let congregation think "Help!"*) Did anyone hear that? (*Let children respond.*) Why not? (*Let children respond.*)

How do you think God did with our hearing test? Remember, he lives way up in Heaven! (*Let children respond.*) Do you think he could hear us when we whispered? (*Let children respond.*) How about when we just thought the word "help"? (*Let children respond.*)

Which do you think was easier for God to hear, the yell or the thought? (*Let children respond.*)

I have some good news for you. God passed our hearing test with flying colors every time! He heard us yell for help, he heard us whisper it, and he even heard us think it. All three times God could hear us just as if we'd spoken right into his ear.

God is amazing! Psalm 4:3 says, "The Lord will hear when I call to him." Whether we yell, whisper, or just think it, God will hear us and answer our call because he cares about us. As you settle into your seats now, think a prayer of thanks to God. He listens to you and hears you no matter how loudly or softly you speak—and even when you don't speak at all.

INTERACTION OPTIONS

Medium: *Choose three helpers prior to the service. One will sit in the front of the church, one about halfway back, and the other in the back of the church. They will each yell, whisper, and think the word "help" when instructed to do so.*

Low: *Have one of the kids yell, whisper, and think the word "help" when instructed to do so.*

The Lord will hear when I call to him.

Peanut Butter Protection

THEME: God's protection

SCRIPTURE: "Spread your protection over them, that those who love your name may rejoice in you" (Psalm 5:11).

SUPPLIES NEEDED: A knife, bread, peanut butter, and jelly to make a sandwich in front of the kids, and a peanut butter and jelly sandwich for each person in the small group or family.

INTERACTION: *A small group or family walks through eating peanut butter and jelly sandwiches. They talk about how they were going to go on a picnic after church, but couldn't wait to eat.*

Today we're going to talk about God's protection. (*Group or family enters eating their PBJ snacks.*) Hey! What are you doing? (*Helpers say they're going on a picnic after church but couldn't wait to eat their PBJ snacks.*)

Eating a peanut butter and jelly snack in church? Hmm. You know, seeing that snack makes me think of a verse about God's protection. Let me read it to you. Psalm 5:11 says, "Spread your protection over them, that those who love your name may rejoice in you."

Doesn't that make you think of peanut butter and jelly snacks? (*Let kids respond.*) How about you out there in the congregation? Everyone who thought of a peanut butter and jelly snack when I read Psalm 5:11, please stand up. (*Pause.*) I can't believe it! No one thought of a peanut butter and jelly snack!

Well, let me explain. I just happen to have some bread in this bag. Now let's pretend that we're all a piece of bread, OK? Along comes some peanut butter and it gets spread all over us. (*Spread peanut butter on bread.*) Now we're covered with peanut butter.

Next comes some jelly. (*Pull out jelly.*) The jelly gets spread all over the peanut butter. (*Spread jelly.*) But look! The jelly doesn't touch us, the bread, because we're spread with the peanut butter protection.

When we're covered with God's protection, like the bread is covered with the peanut butter, bad things in the world won't touch us in the same way they touch the rest of the world, just like the jelly doesn't touch the bread. It was stopped by the peanut butter. Because even when bad things like crime or hate touch our lives, God helps us handle them by comforting us, and giving us strength. God spreads his protection over our hearts and minds so that we can concentrate on rejoicing in him, even when bad things happen.

Now say the verse, Psalm 5:11, after me and this time you'll probably think of peanut butter and jelly snacks! (*Say the verse in small sections and have the children repeat after you.*) Thank you for being such good listeners!

INTERACTION OPTIONS

Medium: *A volunteer sits in the front row eating a peanut butter and jelly snack. Presenter asks what he is doing. Volunteer says he is eating a PBJ snack. Presenter says that reminds him of Psalm 5:11.*

Low: *Presenter eats a peanut butter and jelly sandwich and tells kids it always reminds him of Psalm 5:11.*

Spread your protection over them, that those who love your name may rejoice in you.

God's Mirror

THEME: Self-esteem

SCRIPTURE: "You made him a little lower than the heavenly beings and crowned him with glory and honor" (Psalm 8:5).

SUPPLIES NEEDED: None

INTERACTION: *A basketball team (five or more people) passes through during the message, giving one player a hard time about losing a game. The team exits, but helper stays behind to talk with you.*

Leader: Hi, kids! Come on up. It's great to see you. (*Basketball team passes through, giving one player grief about losing a game. The team exits, except the ridiculed player, who stays behind to talk.*) Well, hi, (helper's name). You look a little down. Is everything all right?

Helper: I feel like a loser.

Leader: Why?

Helper: Oh, I really blew it at the basketball game last night.

Leader: What happened?

Helper: I had the chance to win the game with the final basket and I missed it, so we lost. I let the whole team down.

Leader: Oh. I'm sorry you had a rough game. But you're not a loser. We all have bad days sometimes.

Kids, have you ever had one of those days when nothing goes right? (*Let kids tell about a hard day.*) On those days, everything you try to do ends up a disaster! How do you feel after a day like that? (*Let kids respond.*) I feel sad and even a little angry or grouchy after a day like that. Sometimes I feel like a loser just like our helper does.

Well, I have good news for you. None of us are losers. Not even once in a while on a bad day. We are never losers! In fact, we're winners even on our worst day, and I can prove it to you. Let's look in our Bibles at what Psalm 8:5 has to say. David is talking to God about people and he says, "You made [them] a little lower than the heavenly beings and crowned [them] with glory and honor." Wow! That sounds pretty impressive!

David said God made us a little lower than the heavenly beings. That means we were created to have a little less power than God's mighty angels! The Bible also tells us we were made in God's image. What does that mean? Do you think that means he made us to look like himself? Or do you think it means that we can act like God? (*Let kids respond.*) We're sort of like God's mirrors. When we are kind to others, and forgive them, we reflect a little bit of what God is like to those around us. Just as mirrors reflect our images, we can reflect the image of God. God must think we're pretty special to make us in his image and make us just a little lower than his angels, don't you think?

David also said God crowned us with glory and honor. What kind of people wear crowns? (*Let kids respond.*) Very important people—like kings and queens—wear crowns. And when people are honored, it means they're being told or shown how special they are. At your birthday party, you're the guest of honor. That means everyone else who comes to the party is there because he or she wants you to know how special you are to them. You are being honored because it's your birthday. God crowned us with glory and honor to remind us we are very special to him.

So even on our worst days, we can feel good, because God made us a little lower than his angels. The next time you feel like a loser, remember no one is a loser to God. After all, he made us to be like him and crowned us with glory and honor.

(*Helper jumps up and shouts, "Wow! God thinks I'm special!" and runs out.*)

INTERACTION OPTIONS

Medium: *Omit basketball team. Use one volunteer to act as if he or she feels like a loser. Proceed with remainder of paragraph one.*

Low: *Presenter acts sad and looks for a verse of encouragement in a Bible. He turns to Psalm 8:5 and is reminded of God's love.*

Staying Inbounds

THEME: Boundaries and rules

SCRIPTURE: "The boundary lines have fallen for me in pleasant places; surely I have a delightful inheritance" (Psalm 16:6).

SUPPLIES NEEDED: Various sports balls, i.e., volleyball, soccer ball, basketball, baseball, tennis ball, football

INTERACTION: *Have a football team come in and start playing a football game.*

(Football team comes in and starts playing a game.)

Hey, what are you guys doing? You're not supposed to be running in the church, much less throwing a ball around and playing a football game!

(Players ask, "Why not?")

Because it's against the rules. This is a church, not a playground. We come here to worship God, not to play around.

(Team apologizes and returns to their seats.)

Boy, I'm glad we got that taken care of. Now, I'd like to show you some things that I brought along today. I want you to try to figure out what's alike about all of them. *(Show the sports balls. Give children time to figure out the connection between all of them.)* These are all balls and they're all used to play a sport or game. But if you think about it, all the sports you play with these balls have something else in common. What do these sports have in common? *(Let children guess.)* All these sports have rules. And even more specifically, they all have boundary lines. The boundary lines tell us when the ball is inbounds or out-of-bounds. What happens in most sports when the ball goes out-of-bounds? *(Let kids respond.)* The game stops for a moment and the ball has to be brought inbounds again.

We're just like these balls. We're involved in a game called life. We have boundaries to stay in and rules to follow.

What would happen if we didn't have boundaries or rules to play by? *(Let chil-*

dren respond.) We might get hurt and everything would be out of control. Just think about a soccer game for a minute. What if there were no boundaries or rules? Someone could start kicking the ball and keep kicking it wherever he or she wanted. Pretty soon that person might not even be on the field anymore! Who knows where he'd end up? Maybe in the next state! That wouldn't be a fun game, would it? A life without rules and boundaries isn't fun either. Boundary lines and rules help us to know what's expected of us and so we can stay out of trouble. When your mom or dad or teachers make you follow the rules, be glad. That means they care about you and want you to be safe.

Psalm 16:6 says, "The boundary lines have fallen for me in pleasant places; surely I have a delightful inheritance." David says that boundary lines are good things that help us to have a bright future. A life of joy is waiting for us if we ask God to help us follow the rules and stay in the boundaries he has set up for us.

INTERACTION OPTIONS

Medium: *Two adults to run in the church throwing a ball back and forth.*

Low: *Omit paragraph one.*

The boundary lines
have fallen for me
in pleasant places.

Say What?

THEME: Bad language

SCRIPTURE: "I have resolved that my mouth will not sin" (Psalm17:3).

SUPPLIES NEEDED: A button, a zipper, a padlock, transparent tape, glue, and a Bible

INTERACTION: *Prior to the service, give a "mouth-closing device" to several different people in the congregation. When you ask the congregation for ideas of ways to keep mouths closed, these people will volunteer their ideas based on what item they were given, and come up to try out their mouth-closing device on a child.*

What happens when you stub your toe? (*Let kids respond.*) Have you ever stubbed your toe and the next thing you knew some really bad words came pouring out of your mouth? The tongue is one of the hardest things to tame. People can train lions and elephants to do tricks, but the tongue is more fierce than any wild animal and harder to train to behave properly. It's important not to use bad language because the Bible tells us to honor God in all we do. Even with our words. So how can we tame this wild beast, the tongue? (*Let kids respond.*)

I have given a few mouth-controlling devices to some of our adult friends. They are going to show us how to use them, but we'll need you to help. Any volunteers? (*If more than one child volunteers, use as many as you have mouth-closing gadgets.*) OK, (name of helper), what kind of mouth-closing device do you have?

(*Helper pulls out the button and moves toward a child.*) A button! Have you ever heard anyone say, "Button your lip"? Let's see if it really works. (*Have helper try to button one of the child volunteer's lips.*) Hmm. How did it work? Not too well because your lip doesn't have a buttonhole to put the button through!

Let's try something else. (*To second helper:*) What do you have in your bag (pocket)? (*Helper pulls out the zipper.*) A zipper! Let's try to "zip your lip." Do you think it will work? (*Helper tries to get zipper to stay on child's mouth.*) It doesn't seem to work very well because it doesn't stay on. Guess we'll have to try something else.

How about a padlock? (*Helper pulls out lock and shouts, "I have a lock!"*) Let's put a lock on our lips so that bad words don't slip out. (*Helper tries to lock child's mouth.*) Nope. That doesn't work either. I told you the mouth was hard to tame, didn't I? So far we haven't found anything that will keep it closed.

I know! How about glue? Let's try to glue (name of child) mouth closed! (*Helper starts to glue child's mouth. Respond to protests by acknowledging it's not good to put glue in or on our mouths. Praise kids for being so smart about such things.*) I guess glue isn't such a good idea after all.

Boy, this is hard! What else could we try? (*Helper pulls out tape.*) Oh, that's a good idea! Tape! Let's try it. (*Helper tapes child's mouth closed.*) That seems to have worked. Can you still talk? (*Child may mumble something.*) He can make sounds, but I can't make out the words, can you? But what if he had something important to say? We wouldn't be able to understand him. I'm sure he says a lot more good things than bad, so maybe the tape isn't the best solution either. (*Helper gently removes the tape from child's mouth.*)

Is there anything else we can use? (*Helper stands up and holds out a Bible.*) A Bible! What do you think you do with that? (*Let kids respond.*) That's right, we have to read the Bible to tame our tongues. We have to fill our minds with good things to get good things to come out when we speak. And we have to try our hardest not to say things we shouldn't. We just have to make up our minds we're not going to say bad things. Psalm 17:3 says, "I have resolved that my mouth will not sin." That means that you're determined not to say things you shouldn't, whether it be unkind words or actual swear words. None of those words should ever come out of your mouth. With God's help you won't need any of these mouth-controlling devices except the Bible. Read it, then pray and ask God to help you tame your tongue and speak in a way that would please him.

INTERACTION OPTIONS

Medium: *Use one volunteer to help you demonstrate the mouth-controlling devices.*

Low: *Show the kids the devices yourself rather than using a helper.*

Little Green Riding Hood?

THEME: God's perfect Word

SCRIPTURE: "As for God, his way is perfect; the word of the Lord is flawless" (Psalm 18:30).

SUPPLIES NEEDED: Two copies of this story to give your helpers

INTERACTION: *Have members of the congregation act out the parts of Little Red Riding Hood and the Big Bad Lion as you read the story.*

I'm going to read you a story this morning that you've all probably heard before. It's called "Little Red Riding Hood." I want you to listen very carefully to see if you notice anything different about it, OK? *(Read the following story.)*

Once there was a little girl who was called "Little Red Riding Hood." People called her that because of a red sweater she always wore.

One day, her teacher sent Red Riding Hood out to take a basket of coal to her rich old auntie, who was very sick. On her way there, she was stopped by a big bad lion who said, "Where are you going?"

"I'm taking this basket of coal to my dear, sick auntie," replied Yellow Riding Hood. And off she skipped through the jungle.

The lion ran off and since he could run faster than Yellow Riding Hood could skip, he got to Auntie's house first. He put Auntie in the garage and put on her clothes so he could fool Blue Riding Hood when she got there.

Soon there was a knock on the door and the lion said in his sickliest auntie voice, "Who is it?"

"It's me, Auntie, Little Green Riding Hood. I've brought you a basket of coal."

"Come in, dear," replied the lion.

Red Riding Hood came in and climbed up on the bed beside the lion she thought was her auntie. "Oh, Auntie," she said. "What long hair you have!"

"All the better to style for you," said the lion, fluffing his mane.

"But Auntie, what big feet you have!"

"All the better for stomping on bugs, my dear," said the lion.

"But Auntie, what long whiskers you have!" said Little Purple Riding Hood.

"All the better to tickle you with!" said the lion. And he tickled Red's nose and she sneezed and sneezed and ran home and lived happily ever after. The end.

Did you notice anything different about that story? (*Let children respond.*) It had some changes in it, didn't it? You might even call those changes mistakes or flaws.

I want to read a Scripture verse for you. You can find it in your Bible in Psalm 18:30. This verse says, "As for God, his way is perfect; the word of the Lord is flawless."

God's Word, the Bible, doesn't have any mistakes. It's always right. It never changes like parts of our story changed. That's why we can trust what the Bible says and always believe it. It shows us the best way to live our lives. God's Word and God's ways are always perfect.

INTERACTION OPTIONS

Medium: *Have a volunteer read the story to the children.*

Low: *Read the story to the children yourself.*

As for God, his way is perfect; the word of the Lord is flawless.

God's Game

THEME: God's creation

SCRIPTURE: "The heavens declare the glory of God; the skies proclaim the work of his hands" (Psalm 19:1).

SUPPLIES NEEDED: A flannel board and cotton balls

INTERACTION: *Have a different person from the congregation make each of the different pictures out of cotton. Or ask a few people prior to the service to think of a picture they've seen in the clouds and share it with the kids at the beginning of the message.*

Have you ever looked up at the clouds and found pictures in them? Sometimes you really have to use your imagination. What are some of the things you've seen in the clouds? (*Let children respond.*) Have you ever seen a picture in the clouds and no one else can see it but you? (*Let children respond.*) How did that make you feel? (*Let children respond.*)

Today our helpers are going to make a few cloud shapes on this board and you tell me if they look like anything to you. Remember, sometimes we may see something different than someone else does. OK? (*Have first helper arrange cotton balls in the shape of an animal.*) Do you see anything? Remember that you have to use your imagination! (*Let children say what it looks like to them. There are no wrong answers!*)

Let's try another one. How about this? (*Have second helper arrange cotton balls into a tree shape.*) What do you see this time? (*Let kids respond.*) You're really good at this!

Let's try one more. (*Have third helper arrange cotton into a stick person.*) What do you see? (*Let kids respond.*) Does it look like a person to you? Let's thank our helpers for helping us this morning. (*Everyone claps.*)

I want to read Psalm 19:1 to you: "The heavens declare the glory of God; the skies proclaim the work of his hands." God made a beautiful world for us to see and enjoy every day. He didn't have to make it beautiful. He could have made everything gray or black. But he wanted us to like what he made and to think of him when we looked at it. So the next time you look at the fluffy, white clouds in the crystal blue sky think about God and how wonderful he is. Maybe he's playing a game with you like we played this morning by moving the clouds into different shapes for you to guess. And if you're the only one who can see the picture, then it's extra special because God made that picture especially to share with you. Thank God for the beautiful clouds he made just for you to enjoy today.

INTERACTION OPTIONS

Medium: *Choose one person from the congregation to make shapes (animal, tree, person) out of cotton balls on the flannel board.*

Low: *Choose a different child to make each of the pictures out of cotton.*

The heavens declare the glory of God; the skies proclaim the work of his hands.

Mmm! Good!

THEME: God's goodness

SCRIPTURE: "Taste and see that the Lord is good; blessed is the man who takes refuge in him" (Psalm 34:8).

SUPPLIES NEEDED: Small candies that you can hand out, and a flower for each child (real or artificial)

INTERACTION: *Before the service, choose a few people from the congregation to tell the kids about their favorite food and/or beautiful thing. Use these same people to hand out the candy and flowers during and at the end of the message.*

What is the best thing you have ever tasted? (*Let children respond.*) Wow! Why do you like those things so much? (*Let children respond.*) Makes me hungry just hearing about it! What is the most beautiful thing you have ever seen? (*Let children respond.*) Mmm. They sound absolutely gorgeous! I've chosen a few adults from the congregation to tell us about some of their favorite things. Let's listen to what our adult friends have to say. I wonder if any of their favorites will be the same as the ones you've mentioned! (*When they are finished:*) Boy! There are so many beautiful and tasty things in the world, aren't there? One of my favorite tasty things is candy, and I just happen to have some with me today. Everyone who would like a piece, stand up and clap your hands. (*Have helpers give a piece of candy to each child and have them sit back down.*) Mmm. How does it taste? (*Let children respond.*)

One of my favorite beautiful things is a flower. (*Show flowers.*) They look so pretty and smell so good. And I love the way their petals feel so soft and velvety. But you know what? As yummy as candy is and as beautiful as flowers are, there's something that's even better. Do you know what it is? (*Let children respond.*) God's goodness to us is even better than all the candy in the whole world and more beautiful than the most beautiful field of wildflowers ever grown.

In Psalm 34:8 David says, "Taste and see that the Lord is good; blessed is the man who takes refuge in him." That's what we've done today. We've thought about God's goodness by tasting and seeing some wonderful things he has given us. What does it mean to take refuge in God? (*Let children respond.*) We take refuge in God by trusting him to take care of us and by asking for his help when we need it. I'm going to give you each a flower to remind you of how good God is. Whenever you see something beautiful or taste something really good, remember to thank God for his goodness.

INTERACTION OPTIONS

Medium: *Have just one person share with the children and hand out the candy and flowers.*

Low: *Hand out candy and flowers yourself.*

Taste and see that the Lord is good; blessed is the man who takes refuge in him.

Attention, Life Lovers!

THEME: Making your speech pleasing to God

SCRIPTURE: "Whoever of you loves life and desires to see many good days, keep your tongue from evil and your lips from speaking lies" (Psalm 34:12, 13).

SUPPLIES NEEDED: None

INTERACTION: *A group of people to walk through talking bad about someone. One person to act as spokesman for the group.*

(Group of people walk through talking bad about someone.)

Leader: Wait a minute. Are you sure those things you said about that person are true?

Group: Well, that's what everyone is saying, so I suppose it's true.

Leader: But do you know it to be true?

Group: Well, no.

I think we need to talk about this. Why don't you sit down with us? What do you think, kids? Should we talk badly about people? *(Let kids respond.)* Why or why not? *(Let kids respond.)* Sometimes we may hear something about someone and believe it, but it turns out not to be true. What can happen when we do that? *(Let kids respond.)* The things we say should be pleasing to God. Is that easy to do? *(Let kids respond.)* Not always, is it? Why not? *(Let kids respond.)* Sometimes the people around us at school or wherever we might be may say things they shouldn't. It's only natural to want to fit in and be accepted by people, but we shouldn't do what they do or talk like they talk if it isn't pleasing to God.

How many of you love life? *(Let kids respond.)* Would you rather have lots of good days or lots of bad days in your life? *(Let kids respond.)* Sure, we all enjoy good days. Well, I know just the thing to help you have lots of good days. Psalm 34:12,13, says, "Whoever of you loves life and desires to see many good days, keep your tongue from evil and your lips from speaking lies." In these verses David is saying that if we love life and want to see lots of good days, we shouldn't speak evil or lie. It doesn't matter where we are or who we're with. Whatever we say should be kind, truthful, and clean. What do I mean when I say clean? (*Let kids respond.*) That's right, no dirty jokes, rude comments, bad words, or any ugly language like that.

So remember, the secret to having lots of good days is in your mouth. Your tongue can speak good things or bad. Choose to speak good so you can enjoy life and all the good days it will bring.

INTERACTION OPTIONS

Medium: *Have one person come to you saying bad things about someone.*

Low: *Ask the kids if anyone has ever said something bad about them. Ask them how that felt. Proceed with paragraph two.*

Keep your tongue from evil and your lips from speaking lies.

Mending a Broken Heart

THEME: Sadness

SCRIPTURE: "The Lord is close to the brokenhearted and saves those who are crushed in spirit" (Psalm 34:18).

SUPPLIES NEEDED: A box of tissues, running shoes, a telephone (real or a toy), a Bible

INTERACTION: *Prior to the service, give each of the items listed above to different people in the congregation. During your presentation, you will ask the congregation what they do to feel better when they're sad, and the people you've given items to will stand, show their item, and tell what they do with it.*

Hi, kids! How are you today? Are you feeling happy and full of energy? (*Let kids respond.*) I'm glad you're feeling good today. Do you always feel good, or are there days when you feel a little bit sad? (*Let kids respond.*) Have you ever felt so sad that you thought your heart would break? (*Let kids respond.*) What made you feel that way? (*Let kids respond.*)

Sometimes things happen in our lives that make us feel brokenhearted. Perhaps someone you loved very much died, or maybe there was a divorce in your family, or perhaps your best friend moved away. There are many things that can make us feel very sad, even brokenhearted.

When you feel really sad, what are some things you do to try to feel better? (*Let kids respond.*) Let's find out what some people in our church do when they feel sad.

(*To congregation:*) What do you do to feel better when you feel really sad? (*First helper stands and shows his or her box of tissues, saying he or she has a good cry.*)

Sometimes when you're very sad you might cry. Why would that help you feel better? (*Let kids respond.*) Yes, it helps to have a good cry sometimes to get rid of all that emotion and tension you feel inside. You can use the tissues to blow your nose and to wipe away tears. What else might someone do to feel better? (*Second helper holds up running shoes, saying he or she goes for a jog.*)

Why would jogging help you feel better when you are sad? (*Let kids respond.*) That's right, going out and getting some exercise can make you feel better and help work the stress out of your body. That's a very healthy way to feel better.

(*Third helper holds up a telephone and says he or she calls a friend.*) How can calling a friend make you feel better when you are sad? (*Let kids give their ideas.*) Yes, when you're feeling sad, it can really help to talk to a friend about it, either on the phone or in person.

Does anyone else in the congregation have an idea of how to feel better when you're sad?

(*Fourth helper holds up the Bible and says he or she likes to read God's Word to feel better.*) Hmm. That's interesting! How can the Bible help us when we're feeling sad? (*Let kids respond.*) The Bible is the best help of all. God's Word reminds us that God is always with us and his Holy Spirit is our comforter and guide. The Bible gives us strength and courage. Its words give us hope and encouragement.

Psalm 34:18 says, "The Lord is close to the brokenhearted and saves those who are crushed in spirit." When you're sad, reminding yourself that God is close to you can help you feel better. He really cares about you and is especially close when you're sad. So remember to read God's Word, the Bible, when you're sad, and pray about your sadness. God will hear you, comfort you, and give you the strength you need to get through the tough times.

INTERACTION OPTIONS

Medium: *Have someone show the kids the items and let them guess how these things can be used to make them feel better when they're sad.*

Low: *Show the items yourself and let kids guess their benefit.*

The Lord is close to the brokenhearted and saves those who are crushed in spirit.

How High Can You Reach?

THEME: God's love

SCRIPTURE: "Your love, O Lord, reaches to the heavens, your faithfulness to the skies" (Psalm 36:5).

SUPPLIES NEEDED: Any object that can be held up high (a ball, etc.)

INTERACTION: *Use three different helpers to hold the object. Use a short helper to hold it low, a medium-sized helper to hold it a little higher, and a tall helper to hold the object out of the kids' reach.*

We're going to do an experiment today to see how high we can reach. Who would like to help me? (*Select two or three kids who are of different heights.*)

My helpers are going to hold a _____ and I want you to see if you can reach it, OK? (*Short helper holds object down low enough for all the kids to reach.*) You were all able to reach that, weren't you?

All right, now let's have another helper hold the _____ up a little higher and see if you can still reach it. (*Medium helper holds it higher. The smallest child won't be able to reach it.*) What was that like? (*Let kids respond.*) Were you still able to reach it? Some of you were and some of you weren't. Why weren't some of you able to reach it? (*Let kids respond.*) That's right, the kids who could reach it are taller and can reach higher.

OK, let's try it one more time. (*Tall helper holds object up over his or her head, out of children's reach.*) See if you can reach that! (*Let kids have fun trying.*) What's the matter? (*Let kids respond.*) There are some things that are just too high for us to reach. Even adults can't reach everything. We have to use ladders for jobs like changing lightbulbs in high places, or doing a job up on the roof. Thank you for your help, kids and helpers. You can sit down now.

There's a fun game called "I love you this much." It's a good game to play with your parents or anyone else you love a lot. It goes like this. One person says something like "I love you as much as there are leaves on a tree." Then the other person has to say some thing that tells how much he loves you, like "I love you more than all the bricks in all the buildings in all the world." Or you can say, "I love you as high as I can reach," or "as high as that tree," and so on. You keep going back and forth like that until someone gives up. That's a fun game to play because everyone wins. Everyone feels good even if he or she can't think of some-thing to say back and the game ends.

Do you know how much God loves us? Psalm 36:5 tells us. It says, "Your love, O Lord, reaches to the heavens, your faithfulness to the skies." God's love for us isn't just this high (*hold object down low*), or this high (*hold object at medium height*), or even this high (*hold object over your head*). God's love reaches clear up to the heavens. His faithfulness reaches to the skies. That's a lot of love!

Think about these questions. How far does your love reach? Does it reach only to your family and friends? Or does it reach way out to those in need you don't even know? People need lots of things. We need friends, food, and encouragement. You can tell how much God's love lives in your heart by how far your love reaches.

This week I want you to notice how far your love reaches. If you need to, make some changes in your life so your love will reach to people who need to feel God's love.

INTERACTION OPTIONS

Medium: *Use one person to hold the object at different heights to see if the kids can reach it.*

Low: *Hold the object yourself instead of using a helper.*

Your love, O Lord, reaches to the heavens, your faithfulness to the skies.

Hurry Up, God!

THEME: Waiting

SCRIPTURE: "Be still before the Lord and wait patiently for him" (Psalm 37:7).

SUPPLIES NEEDED: None

INTERACTION: *Three helpers—one to act as a parent, one to act as a child, and the other to act as the parent's friend.*

Today we're going to talk about waiting. There are two kinds of waiting. One is noisy waiting and the other is quiet waiting.

I have three helpers this morning who are going to show you both kinds of waiting. After they're done, I want you to tell me which kind of waiting they showed us. Are you ready? (*Helpers act out a scene of a parent running into a friend at the store. The child becomes rude and impatient while waiting for adults to finish chatting.*) What do you think? Was that noisy waiting or quiet waiting? (*Let children respond.*) Have you ever felt like that child did? We all have. What do you think about the noisy way he waited? (*Let kids respond.*) Sometimes it's hard to know what to do when you're feeling impatient. Let's watch our helpers show us quiet waiting and maybe we'll learn a better way to act when we feel impatient and tired of waiting. (*Helpers replay the same scene, but this time the child waits for a pause in the conversation and says, "Excuse me, Mommy, but I'm getting tired. Can we go home soon?"*)

What made this different from the noisy waiting? (*Let kids respond.*) The child didn't interrupt the adults. He waited to speak until he heard the adults stop talking for a moment. Then he used good manners by saying "excuse me," he spoke respectfully to his mother by saying how he felt, and he offered a good suggestion for how she could help him feel better. Which kind of waiting do you think pleases God the most? (*Let children respond.*)

Psalm 37:7 says, "Be still before the Lord and wait patiently for him." What do you think that Bible verse means? (*Let kids respond.*) It's telling us to be quiet waiters instead of noisy ones. What are some reasons we might have to quietly wait on

31

God? (*Let children respond.*) We wait on God when we pray and don't get an answer right away. We wait on God to take us to Heaven where there won't be any more sadness, sickness, death, or crime. We wait on God when we feel very sad or lonely and we don't feel like he's with us. Sometimes God lets us wait so he can see if we really trust in him. He wants to see if we'll be noisy or quiet waiters.

So the next time you find yourself waiting, remember God is with you, and with his help, you can be a quiet, patient waiter.

INTERACTION OPTIONS

Medium: *Have one helper act out examples of waiting by playing the part of the child after you have verbally explained the scene for the kids.*

Low: *Rather than acting out the examples, simply explain the two types of waiting.*

Be still before the Lord and wait patiently for him.

A Meek Peek

THEME: Meekness

SCRIPTURE: "The meek will inherit the land and enjoy great peace" (Psalm 37:11).

SUPPLIES NEEDED: None

INTERACTION: *Tell the kids you are going to be talking about anger today. Ask the congregation if they have ever been angry. Ask everyone who has ever been angry to please stand.*

We're going to be talking about anger today. Do you ever get angry? What makes you angry? (*Let kids respond.*) (*To the congregation:*) Do you ever get angry? If you've ever been angry, will you please stand up? Wow! Looks like everyone gets mad from time to time. Thank you, you may be seated.

Have you ever known peope who get mad over every little thing? Their feelings are always getting hurt. What's it like being friends with someone like that? (*Let kids respond.*) It's hard to be friends with people like that because no matter how hard you try, they still find something wrong with what you did, and they're mad again.

Are you ever that way? I'm afraid all of us can be that way if we're not careful. What would it be like to be angry all the time? (*Let kids answer.*) Being angry all the time isn't a very fun way to live. What does it feel like to be angry? (*Let kids respond.*) Anger gives us an uneasy feeling inside because we're afraid of the way things could turn out. For instance, suppose I got mad at someone because he or she didn't say hello to me. What might I be afraid of? (*Let kids respond.*) I might be afraid that he or she doesn't like me. I don't like it when people don't like me.

Psalm 37:11 says, "The meek will inherit the land and enjoy great peace." What does it mean to be meek? (*Let kids respond.*) When people are meek, they don't get angry easily. They're patient, kind, and gentle. They think of other peoples' needs before their own. They are the kind of people God will have in his kingdom someday. And what a peaceful way to live! None of that creepy feeling inside like when you're angry.

Getting angry isn't wrong. We all get angry sometimes. But getting angry over all the little things that happen every day is wrong. Why would that be wrong? (*Let kids respond.*) Because then you're not thinking about God anymore. You're thinking about yourself and what you want people to do for you.

So how can you become meek? (*Let kids respond.*) That's right, by thinking more about God and what you can do for others and less about yourself. Then you'll grow into a person who pleases God more every day.

INTERACTION OPTIONS

Medium: *Choose two or three people to share with the kids something that makes them angry.*

Low: *Omit helper involvement. Just talk to the kids about what makes them angry.*

The meek will inherit the land and enjoy great peace.

Watch Your Step!

THEME: Standing firm

SCRIPTURE: "If the Lord delights in a man's way, he makes his steps firm; though he stumble, he will not fall, for the Lord upholds him with his hand" (Psalm 37:23, 24).

SUPPLIES NEEDED: None

INTERACTION: *Ask parents to bring their babies to demonstrate their different levels of mobility: i.e., crawling, walking with hands being held, just starting to walk on their own, and running. The parents will need to encourage the children to move.*

Have you ever seen a little baby just learning to walk? I've invited several parents and their babies to come up to show us how a baby learns to walk.

(Parents and babies come up. Beginning with the youngest baby, each set of parents shows what their baby can do.)

Did you notice that these parents had to hold their baby's hands? What do you think would happen if they let go? *(Let children respond.)* The baby would probably fall. Babies fall down a lot as they learn to walk. But if their daddy or mommy holds their hands, they don't fall because they're being held up. *(To parents and babies:)* Thank you for helping us today. You may return to your seats.

Did you know that's exactly what God does for us? Psalm 37:23, 24 says, "If the Lord delights in a man's way, he makes his steps firm; though he stumble, he will not fall, for the Lord upholds him with his hand." God holds our hands while we learn to live a Christian life, just like a parent holds a baby's hands to help him learn to walk. He doesn't let us fall because he loves us.

So how can we delight the Lord? *(Let children respond.)* By living our best for him. When we think about doing something we shouldn't, we can ask God to help us not do it. We can be kind and helpful to others like Jesus was. We can read our Bibles to learn more about God. These are things that delight God.

Maybe you're wondering, "Why do I still make mistakes and sin even though I'm a Christian?" It isn't because God lets you fall. Remember that God loves you and doesn't like to see you get hurt. We sin because we let go of God's hands when he's trying to help us learn to walk. What would happen if the baby let go of his or her parents' hands? (Let kids respond.) We fall, too, if we let go of God's hands. He wants to hold us up, but he can't if we keep jerking our hands away from his. When we decide to sin and do things our own way, we let go of God's hands and that's when we fall. So hang on tight to God's hands. It's a lot better than falling!

INTERACTION OPTIONS

Medium: *Have one set of parents come up with their baby to demonstrate how a baby learns to walk.*

Low: *Talk with the kids about how babies learn to walk. Or bring in pictures, a home movie, or a video of a baby learning to walk.*

Though he stumble, he will not fall, for the Lord upholds him with his hand.

Blameless? Who, Me?

THEME: Learning from other Christians

SCRIPTURE: "Consider the blameless, observe the upright; there is a future for the man of peace" (Psalm 37:37).

SUPPLIES NEEDED: An 8 ½" x 11" piece of paper for each child

INTERACTION: *Have a few paper airplanes of different styles made ahead of time. (You can get books on making paper airplanes at your local library.) Have one or two planes that don't fly well. Have members of the congregation come up and demonstrate how to fly the paper airplanes, each claiming his or her technique is superior to all others. Have them ham it up, exaggerating each step involved in flying their planes. Choose one person ahead of time to teach the kids how to make a paper airplane. Talk about how they can learn to make paper airplanes.*

Good morning, kids! We're going to learn something today I think you'll find a lot of fun. I have several helpers who are going to show you how to make and fly a paper airplane. I'll give you each a piece of paper and you can learn how to make one, but first, let's have our helpers come up and give us a demonstration of how great these planes can fly. (*Have each helper fly his plane.*)

It seems some of the planes fly better than others. If these were real airplanes, which one would you want to fly on? (*Let kids respond.*) Why? (*Let kids respond.*) Let's have (name of helper) teach us how to make a paper airplane. And let's have the other helpers stay close by in case any of you need help. You'll need to watch (name of helper) very closely and think about what he says so your paper airplane will turn out right. (*Helper teaches kids how to make a paper airplane slowly, fold by fold.*) How did your planes come out? They look great! How did you learn to make them? (*Let kids respond.*) You listened to the instructions and watched how our helper folded his paper. You had to think about what he said, watch how he did it, and then do it. Let's all set our airplanes down for a moment.

There are lots of things you can learn by listening to others, watching what they do, and thinking about how they do it. The Bible tells us in Psalm 37:37 that we should watch other Christians so we can learn to be better followers of Jesus. In this verse, David tells us to "Consider the blameless, observe the upright; there is a future for the man of peace."

Who are the blameless? (Let kids respond.) They're people you can't blame things on because they stay out of trouble and everyone knows it. An upright person is someone we respect because he or she always tries to do what is right.

The last part of verse 37 says, "there is a future for the man of peace." When we are blameless and upright, our lives are much happier and more peaceful. We don't find ourselves in the middle of trouble and bad situations.

We can learn to be blameless and upright by watching people who have been Christians for a long time. Our verse said to "consider the blameless." That means think about them and how they behave. And "observe the upright" means to watch them. How do they live their lives? How do they handle tough situations? How do they talk to people? Older Christians have had a longer time to practice being blameless and upright, so they're better at it than we are. They've also made lots of mistakes and can help us not to make those same mistakes. We become better Christians by watching others and thinking about how they live a Christian life. Then we can try it ourselves. By living the best we can for Jesus, God promises a bright and peaceful future.

INTERACTION OPTIONS

Medium: *Someone to teach the kids how to make a paper airplane. A few extra helpers to help some of the younger kids fold their paper into an airplane.*

Low: *Fold the paper airplane yourself. Ask kids how they could best learn to make a paper airplane.*

The Never-Ending Gift

THEME: God's gift of salvation

SCRIPTURE: "The salvation of the righteous comes from the Lord; he is their stronghold in time of trouble" (Psalm 37:39).

SUPPLIES NEEDED: A small gift-wrapped box to give each child.

INTERACTION: *Earlier in the week, ask a few members of the congregation to tell about or bring in one of their favorite gifts.*

Hi, kids! It's so good to see you this morning. We're going to talk about gifts today. Have you ever gotten a gift you liked so much you still remember it? What is the best gift you've ever received? *(Let kids respond.)* Wow! Those sound like wonderful gifts. I can see why you still remember them. What about some of you adults in the congregation? What are some of your most memorable gifts? *(Let helpers stand and tell about their gifts.)*

I know another gift that's worth remembering. It's the gift of salvation. What is salvation? *(Let kids respond.)* It's when you're saved from something. When God saves us from a life of sin, and saves us from having to pay for our sins, he has given us salvation.

When you buy a gift for someone, you have to go to a store and pay whatever the price tag shows. The Bible tells us the price of sin is death. We deserve to die because we're so sinful. But God paid for our sin by having Jesus die on a cross for us so we don't have to die. All we have to do is receive the gift of salvation.

But how do you receive this gift that you can't even see? *(Let kids respond.)* By believing that Jesus is the Son of God, and asking him to be your Savior. Then we try to do what God asks us to do, and live our lives the way he would want us to live. When we give our lives to Jesus, God promises another gift: eternal life. What is that? *(Let kids respond.)* That means someday we'll live forever in Heaven with God!

Psalm 37:39 says, "The salvation of the righteous comes from the Lord; he is their stronghold in time of trouble." That means that when we accept God's gift of salvation, he will help us stay strong in our times of trouble. And he gives us ever-lasting life. Wow! That's a great gift.

I brought each of you a little gift-wrapped box today to remind you of God's wonderful gift. There's nothing inside because God's gift is too great to fit in a box. Maybe you can put your reminder gift somewhere in your room where you'll see it all the time. Whenever you see it, remember to thank God for his gift of salvation. If you haven't accepted God's gift of salvation yet, you can do it today. If you have questions about it, talk to your mom or dad, your Sunday school teacher, any of the ministers, or me, and we will be glad to help you find the answers in God's Word. Salvation is a gift you'll definitely add to the top of your best gifts list!

INTERACTION OPTIONS

Medium: *Someone to interrupt your message early on to give you a present. Thank her for the wonderful surprise, and ask if you can open it later. Helper agrees, and returns to her seat. Proceed with paragraph one, omitting congregation involvement.*

Low: *Talk to the kids about their favorite gifts, but omit congregation involvement.*

The salvation of the righteous comes from the Lord.

It's Too Heavy!

THEME: Guilt

SCRIPTURE: "My guilt has overwhelmed me like a burden too heavy to bear" (Psalm 38:4).

SUPPLIES NEEDED: A box of books or anything else that would be too heavy for a child to carry.

INTERACTION: *Two or three men to carry the box in to donate the contents to the church.*

Hi, kids! How are you today? (*Helpers struggle down the aisle with the heavy box, saying they have some things they'd like to donate to the church.*) Well, how nice! Thank you. Let's see, why don't you just give that box to one of these kids and he will take it to the other room. How about if you give it to (name one of the smallest kids)? (*Kids will probably protest saying that the box is too heavy for him.*) What? You don't think (name) can carry that box? (*Let kids respond.*) Why not? (*Let kids respond. Say to child:*) You may be very strong, but that box is just too heavy to carry. (*To helpers:*) Why don't you just set the box right here? We may be able to use it during our children's message.

Boy, that box sure looks heavy. I'm glad you didn't have to lift it. You know, there is something you can carry around that's even heavier than that box. Do you know what it is? (*Let children guess.*) It's guilt. Who can help explain what guilt is? (*Let kids respond.*) Guilt can weigh you down even more than a heavy box of books. It can take over your life so much you don't even know what to do about it anymore. We all do things we're ashamed of and that's when we feel guilty. The Bible tells us that David felt that way. In Psalm 38:4, David said, "My guilt has overwhelmed me like a burden too heavy to bear." David felt so bad about something he had done he didn't know what to do. Have you ever felt that way? (*Let kids respond.*)

(*Point to box.*) How can we make this box lighter? (*Let kids respond.*) That's right, by taking the books out. Will you help me take all these books out of the

41

box? (*Kids help empty the box.*) There. That should make it more manageable. Let's have (name of child) try to lift it now! (*Let child lift box.*) There's a solution to that yucky guilty feeling too. What should we do when we feel that way? (*Let kids respond.*) We can pray and ask God to forgive us for what we did. How do you think God feels when we admit that we did something wrong and ask him to forgive us? (*Let kids respond.*) God loves to forgive his children. He's always glad when we come to him and admit that we sinned and then ask for his forgiveness. Why do you think that makes God happy? (*Let kids respond.*) Because it shows that we love him and want to live a life that pleases him.

If we feel guilty because we hurt someone, what else should we do besides ask God to forgive us? (*Let kids respond.*) It's important to go to the person we hurt and tell her that we're sorry, too. Why should we do that? (*Let kids respond.*) Saying we're sorry makes it easier to go on being friends with people when we make mistakes. By apologizing to the people we hurt, and admitting our sin to God, we unload our heavy guilt, just like taking books out of this box makes it lighter.

So remember, when you get that heavy, guilty feeling, you don't have to keep feeling that way. You can tell God you're sorry and ask him to help you do what's right the next time, and you can apologize to your friend so your burden doesn't get too heavy to carry.

INTERACTION OPTIONS.
Medium: *Have one person carry in the box for you.*
    Low: *Have the box of books up front already and ask one of the kids to move it out of the way.*

My guilt has overwhelmed me like a burden too heavy to bear.

Live It Up!

THEME: Life is short; live it well

SCRIPTURE: "You have made my days a mere handbreadth; the span of my years is as nothing before you. Each man's life is but a breath" (Psalm 39:5).

SUPPLIES NEEDED: None

INTERACTION: *Involve older members of your congregation by having everyone over the age of seventy stand. If some are unable to stand, have someone next to them stand on their behalf. Have everyone under the age of eighty sit down. Then ask everyone under the age of ninety to sit. Repeat this process until only the oldest person(s) in the congregation is standing. Ask him or her if it's true that time passes faster the older you get. Give the older members a round of applause for their steadfast faith through the years.*

Begin this message by having the older adults stand, as explained in the interaction above. After the applause, continue as follows.

How many of you think it takes a long time for Christmas to come each year? (*Let kids raise their hands.*) What other things take a long time? (*Let kids respond.*) When you're young, time passes very slowly. It can seem like Christmas—or your birthday—will never come! But as you grow older, time passes faster. So by the time you're ninety, it probably seems like Christmas comes about once a month! How long do you think it will take until you're very old? Do you think it will take this long? (*Hold your hands a few inches apart.*) Or this long? (*Spread your arms out wide.*) How long do you think it will take? (*Let kids show you.*) Let's all look at our hands. How wide is your hand? (*Let kids respond.*) Now let's all take a deep breath and let it out. How long did that take? (*Let kids respond.*) That's how long our lives really are.

In Psalm 39:5 David says, "You have made my days a mere handbreadth; the span of my years is as nothing before you. Each man's life is but a breath." That means that to God, our lives are only as long as our hands are wide, or as long as it takes to take a breath. Even though our lives may seem long to us, they seem very short to God because he has been alive forever. There is nothing for us to worry about or feel sad about because God gives us each day to enjoy. He knows that our lives seem long to us. He wants to use each day to show us his love and give us his blessings.

Compared to God, we're alive on this earth for only a short time. We get only one chance to live this life and we should try to live it in a way that makes God happy. How do we do that? *(Let kids respond.)* That's right—by loving those around us, being kind to others, sharing what we have with those in need, and by telling others of God's love for them. Our lives may seem long to us, but remember, we have only one life to live for God. Let's live it our very best.

INTERACTION OPTIONS

Medium: *Find out ahead of time who is the oldest person in your congregation. Tell him or her prior to the service that you would like him or her to stand when asked to, tell his or her age, and tell whether or not time passes faster the older you get.*

Low: *Tell the kids you've heard that time goes more quickly as you get older. Proceed with paragraph one.*

Each man's life is but a breath.

44

Looking Ahead

THEME: Jesus' return

SCRIPTURE: "But now, Lord, what do I look for? My hope is in you" (Psalm 39:7).

SUPPLIES NEEDED: None

INTERACTION: *Several people who are planning a church activity or program walk through talking about how they are looking forward to this event and can't wait until it gets here. (This can be an opportunity to promote such an event also!)*

(People walk through talking about how much they are looking forward to an upcoming church event.) That sounds like fun! They are really looking forward to _____ , aren't they? I hope you and your families can be there to enjoy it too. What are some things you look forward to? *(Let kids respond.)* I can see why you look forward to those things; they sound wonderful! Have you ever looked forward to something so much you thought about it all the time? You may have planned for it, dreamed about it, and even marked the days off on the calendar until the special day finally arrived.

Sometimes I feel a little sad if nothing exciting is coming up. My birthday may have just come and gone, or vacation is over, and there's just nothing to look forward to. Do you ever feel that way? *(Let kids respond.)* King David did. In Psalm 39:7 he wrote, "But now, Lord, what do I look for? My hope is in you." He asked God what there was to look forward to. And then David answered his own question; he said his hope was in God.

Christians always have something to look forward to. It's better than birthdays, Christmas, or vacations, and it will last forever. Do you know what it is? *(Let children respond if they want.)* One day Jesus will come back to earth. The Bible tells us a special instrument will be blown to signal his return. Can you guess what instrument it will be? *(Let children guess.)* In 1 Thessalonians 4:16 Paul, Silas, and Timothy tell us that "the Lord himself will come down from heaven, with a loud command, with the voice of the archangel and with the trumpet call of God." What do you think it will be like when Jesus comes again? *(Let kids respond.)* We'll all live with him forever in peace and love. There won't be any more sickness, death, or sadness when he returns. All the bad things we have to put up with in this world will be gone. That's something we can look forward to just like David did. If we put our hope in God we'll never be disappointed, and we'll always have something to look forward to.

INTERACTION OPTIONS

Medium: *Someone to act discouraged because he or she doesn't have anything to look forward to now that his or her birthday has passed.*

Low: *Omit helper involvement. Begin by asking kids what they look forward to.*

But now, Lord, what do I look for? My hope is in you.

Eu! Slimy!

THEME: God is our Rock

SCRIPTURE: "He lifted me out of the slimy pit, out of the mud and mire; he set my feet on a rock and gave me a firm place to stand" (Psalm 40:2).

SUPPLIES NEEDED: A rock that will fit in one hand to give each child.

INTERACTION: *Someone to volunteer to lead the children on two imaginary hikes—one through mud and mire, the other through dry land with large rocks. Invite members of the congregation who love the outdoors to join you.*

We're going to do some hiking today. It will be imaginary hiking, but we'll have lots of fun. So get ready! My helper will be guiding us on two hikes. The first, I should warn you, will be a little messy. It will be through lots of slippery, muddy areas. Are you ready? OK, lead the way, helper. *(Helper leads children on a short, imaginary hike in the church within view of the congregation. He narrates as he leads, such as, "Watch out for this big puddle here. You'll have to jump across it. It's muddy on the other side, so try not to slip and fall." Helper jumps, slips, waves his arms wildly to keep his balance. "Whew! That was close!" Helper waits as each child jumps the puddle and regains his balance. Helper continues the hike in this manner for a couple of minutes and then leads the children back to where they started.)*

What an exciting hike that was! I thought you were all going down in the mud at that one point! It's hard to keep from slipping when you're walking in mud and water, isn't it?

We'd better get started on our second hike right away. This time we're going to go hiking where there are lots of rocks to climb and no mud. Show us the way, (name)! *(Helper takes kids on imaginary hike, climbing on rocks. He points out good places for them to put their feet to get good, solid footing. Praise ther   uch good hiking and climbing skills. At the end, they all should be standing   imaginary rock together, enjoying a beautiful view.)*

Oh, what a wonderful hike! Thank you for taking us, (name)! Let's all go back and sit down a minute and talk about our hikes. *(Helper returns to his seat and kids follow you to where you normally give the message.)* Which one was easier? The slippery, muddy hike or the one where you had good, solid rocks to walk on? *(Let kids respond. Be prepared! Some may like the antics of slipping through mud better than standing on rocks! All answers are acceptable, but make a strong point for the rocks' safe footing as you talk.)*

In our Bibles, I think David knew something about the difference between hiking in mud and hiking on rocks. In Psalm 40:2 he wrote about God, "He lifted me out of the slimy pit, out of the mud and mire; he set my feet on a rock and gave me a firm place to stand." David said that trying to handle a problem without God's help is like being in a slimy pit where he just kept slipping in sin. There's nothing worse than slipping in sin! It's worse than slipping in mud because mud can be easily washed off. But sin makes you feel bad, not just on the outside, but on the inside, too.

But when David gave his problem to God, he said God set his feet on a rock and gave him a firm place to stand. Not a slippery, slimy place. So it was easier for him to live a good life for God and get through tough situations with God's help because he had good, solid footing. God becomes our rock when we trust in him. When we accept Jesus into our lives, he washes away those muddy sins and helps us not to slip in them so much.

I'm going to give each of you a rock to remind you to trust in God. He's our rock in tough times and will give you good footing so you don't fall. When you are faced with a rough situation, you can squeeze your rock in your hand or just remember that God is your rock and remind yourself to hang on tight to him. You'll have a great hike through life if God is your rock!

INTERACTION OPTIONS

Medium: *Lead the kids on the hikes yourself.*

Low: *Talk about hiking through mud and over rocks.*

The Real Thing

THEME: False gods

SCRIPTURE: "Blessed is the man who makes the Lord his trust, who does not look to the proud, to those who turn aside to false gods" (Psalm 40:4).

SUPPLIES NEEDED: Play money

INTERACTION: *Someone who says she wants to buy something from you, and then gives you play money to pay for it. Give the congregation the opportunity to share a real rip-off story or two.*

Leader: Hi, kids! How are you today? It's so good to see all of you.

Helper: *(walking briskly toward you:)* I can't stand it anymore! I just have to have that watch you're wearing! I've been admiring it all morning and I love it so much I want to buy it from you.

Leader: You've got to be kidding! I just got this watch for Christmas *(my birthday)*. I really can't part with it.

Helper: Oh, please. I'll give you one hundred dollars in cash for it right now. It would mean so much to me.

Leader: It would? Well . . . I guess . . . if it would mean that much to you . . . I guess I could always buy another watch. OK, I'll sell it to you for one hundred dollars.

Helper: Oh, thank you! *(She hugs you and gives you her money and starts walking away.)*

Leader: Hey! Wait a minute!

Helper: *(stops)* What?

Leader: This money you just gave me is fake! It's play money!

Helper: So?

Leader: So it's no good. The deal is off. I need my watch back. *(Helper tru~~ ~~ back up front to return the watch to you. You give the play money back, and she~~ ~~ her seat grumbling about "details.")*

Wow, that was a close one! I could have really gotten ripped off if I hadn't looked at that money closely. A lot of things in life are not what they seem to be. Can you think of an ad or commercial that made you think things are different than they really are? A commercial that makes something look much better than it really is? (*Let kids respond. Some examples would be dolls that fly and dance on TV but don't in real life, or shoes that make you run faster.*)

Those things are fake. There are even fake gods. A fake god is anything that becomes more important to you than the real God who created the universe. Can you think of an example of a fake god? What kinds of things do you care the most about? (*Let children respond.*) Friends, TV, having the right clothes, or getting on the team could all be fake gods. Those things that are more important in your life than God are just fake gods. They can't do the same things the real God can do. You can't buy things with fake money and you can't be saved from a life of sin by a fake god.

What does our one, true God do? (*Let kids respond.*) What does God expect from us? (*Let kids respond.*) How do you think God feels when we choose other things to be more important to us than he is? (*Let children respond.*)

God wants to come first and be involved in the things we enjoy. He deserves to come first because he's God. If he doesn't come first, then we've replaced the real God with a fake god in our lives. Only the true God can give us everlasting life and blessings to enjoy in this life. Our friends can't, the TV can't, having nice things and being popular can't. Only God can save us from our sins.

In Psalm 40:4, David wrote, "Blessed is the man who makes the Lord his trust, who does not look to the proud, to those who turn aside to false gods." David said we'll be blessed if we put our trust in God and turn away from fake gods (*hold up fake money*). Don't be fooled by fake things like I was almost fooled by that play money. It's a rip-off to think a fake god can provide the blessings or security we have in the real God. So be on your guard. Don't get ripped off. There's only one real God. He's the only one we can trust with our lives and who deserves our attention.

INTERACTION OPTIONS

Medium: *Someone to try to pay you with play money, but omit congregation rip-off stories.*

Low: *Show the kids some play money. Ask them what they can buy with it. Ask if they would they feel cheated if someone bought something from them and paid them with play money.*

Count Me In

THEME: God's wonders

SCRIPTURE: "Many, O Lord my God, are the wonders you have done. . . . Were I to speak and tell of them, they would be too many to declare" (Psalm 40:5).

SUPPLIES NEEDED: A jar of sand and a jar of pre-counted dry beans.

INTERACTION: *Someone with a jar of sand asks for kids' help in counting the grains of sand. Later, allow members of the congregation and the kids to guess how many beans there are in a jar.*

Hi, kids! How are you today? It's so good to see all of you. My friend, (name), has a problem that she thought perhaps you could help her with. I'll let her explain. (*Helper asks kids how high they can count and lets kids respond. Helper says she hopes that will be high enough because she wants them to help her count the grains of sand in the jar.*) Wait just a minute! That's going to take way too long! Not to mention the mess it would make in our church building. I think you're going to have to find someone else to help with that project. We've got some important things to talk about here today. (*Helper, disappointed, says OK, and walks away.*)

Can you imagine trying to count grains of sand? (*Bring out jar of beans.*) I have a jar of beans here. How many beans do you think there are? (*Let kids guess.*) How about you adults, how many beans do you think there are? (*Call on several members for their answers.*) Well, I counted the beans before church and there are ____ beans. That's a lot of beans, isn't it? Maybe it wouldn't be too bad to count a jar full of beans or sand, but how about a whole beach full of sand? Does that sound like a project you'd like to tackle? (*Let kids respond.*) Why or why not? There are just way too many grains of sand to even begin to count them all. I'd probably lose count and then have to start over again!

In Psalm 40:5 David tells us about something else that is too high
They are the wonders of God. He says, "Many, O Lord my God, are th

you have done. . . . Were I to speak and tell of them, they would be too many to declare." David says he can't even begin to tell about all the wonderful things that God has done because there are just too many to tell. There are so many, that he can't even count them all. No one can count that high because every second God is doing wonderful things. What kind of wonderful things does God do? (*Let kids respond.*) He does things like giving life to a new baby, or causing a flower to bloom, or making rain fall on dry land, or painting a sunset in the sky for us to enjoy. And those are just a few of the wonders that God does for us every day. And how about some of the things God does that we don't even think about? Like making our bones grow? And making our cuts heal? And why is it that the earth is always spinning but we can't even feel it?

What are some wonderful things God does for you? (*Let children respond.*) We certainly have a great God. He loves us so much that he does wonderful things for us every day. Let's bow our heads and take a moment to thank him for his wonders that are so many we can't even count them. (*Say a brief prayer of thanks to God for his love and the wonderful things he does for us each day.*)

INTERACTION OPTIONS

Medium: *Someone to come in with the jar of sand and ask for your help with a project (counting the grains of sand). Omit congregational involvement in guessing how many beans there are.*

Low: *Omit the first paragraph. Begin by showing the kids the jar of sand and asking them if they think they could count how many grains of sand there are. Then show them the jar of beans and let them guess how many there are.*

Many, O Lord my God, are the wonders you have done.

Are You a Kind Person?

THEME: Kindness

SCRIPTURE: "Blessed is he who has regard for the weak; the Lord delivers him in times of trouble" (Psalm 41:1).

SUPPLIES NEEDED: None. Optional: a pair of broken eyeglasses.

INTERACTION: *One person to walk into a wall or trip and fall on something he or she didn't see because his or her glasses are broken. A small group of people will react kindly with concern and another group will react unkindly by laughing.*

(As the kids come up and take their seats, have your visually-challenged helper [helper #1] begin coming up also. Along the way, he trips and falls. The two groups of helpers, who are seated in the congregation, react kindly or unkindly. The kind group jumps up to assist helper #1 and checks to see if he [or she] is all right. The unkind group stands up, points and laughs, and calls helper #1 clumsy. Kind helpers tell them to stop it. Helper #1 says he [or she] broke his [or her] glasses this morning and can't see very well. He [or she] thanks the kind helpers as they all return to their seats.)

Boy, that was too bad that (name) fell down. It's hard to see when your glasses are broken. What was different about the way the two groups of people reacted to (name) falling down? (*Let kids respond.*) That's right; one group was kind and the other was unkind. Tell me about someone you know who is really kind. (*Let kids respond.*) What are some things he or she does that show kindness? (*Let children tell you.*) Those are pretty good ways to tell that a person is kind. How do you know when someone is mean? (*Let kids tell you.*)

It's easy to recognize when someone else is kind, but it's not always as easy for us to be kind. We have to work at thinking of ways to show kindness to others, especially to those who are different from us. In Psalm 41:1 David writes, he who has regard for the weak; the Lord delivers him in times of trouble regard for the weak means protecting those who may not be able to defend themselves, or being willing to assist someone who is smaller than us, or someone whose body won't allow him to do all the things a stronger, healthier person can do. It means being kind to someone who is limited by physical or mental handicaps. We need to show extra kindness to these people. God tells us when we're kind to the weak he will help us in times of trouble.

I want you each to think of someone right now who needs your friendship. It might be someone you're not usually kind to or someone you ignore. (*Pause a moment to let the kids think of someone.*) Now think of one thing that you can do to be kind to him or her. (*Pause again and let children think.*) Your assignment this week is to be kind to that person.

INTERACTION OPTIONS

Medium: *One person to walk into a wall or trip and fall on something he or she couldn't see because his or her glasses are broken. One person to react kindly and another person to react unkindly when he or she falls.*

Low: *Tell a story of someone falling and the two different reactions (kind and unkind) he or she received. Proceed with paragraph two.*

Blessed is he who has regard for the weak.

Hip Hip Hooray!

THEME: Praising God

SCRIPTURE: "Clap your hands, all you nations; shout to God with cries of joy" (Psalm 47:1).

SUPPLIES NEEDED: None

INTERACTION: *Cheerleaders in the congregation are invited to come up and help lead a praise cheer for God. The entire congregation will participate in the wave.*

Have you ever gone to a sports event or a concert where there was a crowd of people who were excited about what was happening? (*Let children respond.*) What was that like? (*Let children tell about where they were and what it was like.*) It's exciting to be a part of a crowd at a special event, isn't it? You can just feel the energy coming from all the people. You're all there for the same reason—you like sports or music and you're excited for your show to begin. And when it does, you stand and cheer and yell and clap your hands. Some people are really good at whistling—they whistle so loud that you have to cover your ears! Are any of you good at whistling? (*If so, ask several children to come demonstrate their whistles.*)

Every week we have a chance to be part of an excited crowd who comes together for the same reason. We come together to praise and worship God. Can you think of some reasons to praise God? (*Let kids respond.*) What are some things he has done for us? (*Let kids respond.*) What are some words that tell us what God is like? (*Let kids respond.*) Those things are way more exciting and important than a touchdown. (*With growing excitement in your voice:*) And every week we get to be with other people who love God and are excited about what he's done for us! (*To congregation:*) Isn't that right? (*You'll probably get little response from the congregation.*) Hmm. This crowd doesn't seem to be as energized as the crowds I've seen at football games or concerts. Do they seem excited to you, kids? (*Let kids respond.*) We need to do something about that. After all, God is way more deserv[ing of] praise and cheers than football players are. Let's see, what could we do know! Sometimes at games when the crowd seems a little quiet they'll have cheer-leaders who try to perk them up. Maybe that's what we need.

Here's what we'll do. I'll give the congregation an instruction like "yell your loudest," and you help me lead them in that yell. You'll be like the cheerleaders at a game. Remember that cheerleaders have to be louder than the audience so they can get the audience all fired up. Can you do that? I think we're going to need a few cheerleaders from the adults too. *(Have a few adults to help.)*

(To congregation:) Let's begin by giving God a round of applause just to get warmed up. *(Make sure the kids clap along.)* OK, that wasn't too bad. But I know you can do better. This time, let's stand up and clap and whoop a little. Let's give God some yells like at a football game when a touchdown is made. You whistlers might even want to whistle. Remember, God is awesome! Let's really show him how much we love and appreciate all he's done for us. Ready to lead them, kids? Everyone on your feet! Ready, set, cheer! *(Yell and cheer for God.)* Wow! That's more like it.

Hey, I know what else we can do. The wave! Have you ever seen a big crowd of people do the wave at a sports event? It looks really neat, doesn't it? All those peo-ple standing up and lifting their arms over their heads one by one. Let's do a wave for Jesus! We'll start in the front row on this side and go row by row towards the back. When it gets to the back, we'll switch over to the front on the other side of the church and go back with the wave on that side. *(Do the wave. Organize your wave however it will work best at your church.)*

That was great! I bet Jesus is smiling right now. Psalm 47:1 says, "Clap your hands, all you nations; shout to God with cries of joy." So praise God with all your might just like at other events. Let's keep that smile on God's face.

INTERACTION OPTIONS

Medium: *Have "cheerleaders" from the congregation come up and lead cheers for God, but omit the wave.*

Low: *Lead the kids in the wave yourself.*

Mine!

THEME: Sharing

SCRIPTURE: "The world is mine, and all that is in it" (Psalm 50:12).

SUPPLIES NEEDED: Large cookies to share with the kids, but not enough to go around

INTERACTION: *A Sunday school class or Bible study group to bring the cookies to the kids as a special treat. One person to speak for the group.*

(Sunday school class or Bible study group comes in and says:)

Spokesperson: Excuse us, but we brought some cookies to share with these great kids today. Do you mind if we hand them out now while they're all here together?

Leader: Well, how nice of you! No, I don't mind if you hand them out now. That would be wonderful!

Spokesperson: Let me make sure I have enough for everyone." *(S/he looks in the bag as if to count the cookies.)* Oh no! I'm a few cookies short. There aren't enough for everyone! What am I going to do?

Leader: Oh dear. That is a problem. It wouldn't be fair if a few kids didn't get a cookie and everyone else did. Do you kids have any ideas of what we should do? Maybe we can figure out a way to share them. *(Let kids respond.)* Oh! That's a great idea! We can split each cookie in half. That way, everyone would get half a cookie. *(To helper:)* Would you mind splitting the cookies in half?

Spokesperson: No. That would be fine. I'm just glad the kids came up with a solution to my problem. *(Helper hands out half cookies to kids.)*

Leader: Thank you so much!

Spokesperson: You're welcome. I'm glad to share the things God gives me. Well, I've got to go. Hope you enjoy the cookies!

Well, that was a nice surprise, wasn't it? Sometimes sharing is the best way to solve problems. It would have been nice to get a whole cookie, but after all, those cookies weren't ours to begin with. It was nice to get even half a cookie. When I came to church this morning, I didn't expect to get any cookies, so I still ended up getting more than I thought I would!

What are some of your favorite toys? (*Let kids respond.*) Did you know all those favorite toys are only on loan to you for you to take care of and enjoy? God has given us all that we have. That's why we shouldn't be selfish with our things. They're not ours, anyway. So when someone wants to try out our new bike, it's all right. It's good to share the nice things God gives us. In Psalm 50:12 God says, "The world is mine, and all that is in it." I don't think God would want us to be selfish with the things he's provided for us. The Bible says that God owns the cattle on a thousand hills and every animal of the forest, every bird in the mountains and creature of the field. We should share what we have because God is sharing everything with us.

INTERACTION OPTIONS

Medium: *Have one person bring cookies to the kids, rather than a group.*

Low: *Bring the cookies yourself to share with the kids.*

The world is mine, and all that is in it.

Read My Mind

THEME: Our thoughts

SCRIPTURE: "Listen to my prayer, O God, do not ignore my plea; hear me and answer me. My thoughts trouble me and I am distraught" (Psalm 55:1, 2).

SUPPLIES NEEDED: None

INTERACTION: *You'll need two helpers to have their "minds read," and another to do the "mind reading."*

Hello, kids! How are you today? Are any of you feeling extra smart today? (*Let kids respond.*) I wonder if any of you are so smart today that you could read someone's mind? (*Before kids can answer, "mind reader helper" stands up and says, "I feel so smart today that I bet I can read someone's mind."*) Well, I was really asking the kids, but . . . OK, if you're feeling that good about it, let's give it a try. Come on up, (name). (*Helper comes to the front.*) Now I need a volunteer who is willing to have his or her mind read. Who will help us? (*Preselected helper raises his hand.*) Good. (Name) is willing to have his mind read. Come on up here.

All right (name), you think of a number between one and ten, and our mind reader will try to guess what it is. (*Mind reader puts her fingertips on helper's temples while he clenches his jaw a number of times. Mind reader will be able to count the number of jaw clenches by feeling helper's temples move.*) Do you know what the number was? (*Mind reader tells the number.*) Is she right, (name)? (*Yes.*) Wow! That's amazing! Let's try it again. Why don't we have a different person have his mind read? Thank you for helping us, (name). (*First helper returns to seat while you call second helper up. Repeat trick.*) OK, what was the number this time? (*Mind reader gives the number and helper confirms it.*) How do you do that? All right, this time I'm going to have you go way over there, (mind reader), and see if you can read (name's) mind from that distance. (*Mind reader walks away. Helper stays where he is.*) Tell us when you're ready, (name.) (*Helper says he or she is ready. Mind reader closes her eyes and strains to read helper's mind. Then mind reader finally says she thinks she has it and guesses the number.)* Is she right, (name)? *(No.)* No? You mean she didn't read your mind? *(Helper shakes his head.)* So (mind reader's name) can't read your mind from that distance. There must have been a trick for her to be able to read it before. *(Mind reader sheepishly admits she had a trick.)* I must say, it was a very good trick. You had us believing for a minute that you could really read minds. Will you tell us how to do it? *(Mind reader explains the trick. Let kids touch their temples to feel how they move when they clench their jaws.)* Thank you for sharing that with us. That was really fun. *(Helpers return to their seats.)*

You know, we can't really read each other's minds. Sometimes we might be able to guess what someone is thinking. But unless you know a trick like our helper did, that's all it is—a guess. We can't really know for sure. To tell you the truth, I'm glad that people can't read my mind. The things I think aren't always nice and I would hate for anyone else to be able to know what I was thinking. Do you ever feel that way? *(Let kids respond.)*

The things we think are called our "thought life." It's important to think about good things because our thoughts affect the way we live. If we always think mean or selfish things, then chances are we'll be mean or selfish people. Unfortunately that's the way much of our world thinks. But if we think kind and helpful thoughts, it will be easier to be kind and helpful like Jesus was.

Sometimes our thoughts worry us. Thoughts like, "What if I don't pass my test?" or "What if I wreck my bike?" can turn you into a worrywart. A worrywart is a person who worries about things that may never happen. And if you're a worrywart, you're not trusting God. In Psalm 55:1, 2, David says, "Listen to my prayer, O God, do not ignore my plea; hear me and answer me. My thoughts trouble me and I am distraught." David knew he should think good things. He knew he shouldn't worry, but should trust in God. Sometimes that's hard to do.

Your thoughts influence whom you become. If you think on the things of the world, soon you'll be like the world with all its worries and cares. But if you think on the things of God, you'll soon be a fantastic follower of his, trusting in his strength to carry you through any situation. God can always read our minds, so let's give him something good to read.

INTERACTION OPTIONS

Medium: *Read the mind of only one helper.*

Low: *Use only one helper and have him or her read your mind using the trick described.*

In God We Trust

THEME: Fear; trusting God

SCRIPTURE: "In God I trust; I will not be afraid" (Psalm 56:11).

SUPPLIES NEEDED: None

INTERACTION: *Two or three people from the congregation will talk about their fears.*

What are some things you're afraid of? (*Let kids respond.*) Do you want to know what I'm afraid of? (*Share something you're afraid of.*) Everyone has something he or she fears. Even adults. How about some of you in our congregation? What are some of your fears? (*Let helpers respond.*) The fears of older people are different from the fears of kids, aren't they? Why is that? (*Let kids respond.*) As we get older, we learn to live with our fears and sometimes to conquer them. As we trust God with our problems throughout our lives, we also learn that he is always with us. Then our fears don't control our lives.

What do you do when you're afraid? (*Let kids respond.*) Sometimes it helps to have someone with us. Why does that help? (*Let kids respond.*) Yes, you feel less afraid when your mom or dad is with you because you trust her or him to keep you safe. You know your parents love you and wouldn't want you to get hurt or feel afraid. They hold you close and your fear slowly goes away.

But what about if you feel afraid and your mom or dad isn't close by? What do you do then? (*Let kids respond.*) I try to remember that God is always with me even though I can't see him. God is our heavenly Father and he never leaves our side. So when we're afraid and no one is around to help us, we can remember that we're not really alone. How do you think God feels when we're scared? (*Let kids respond.*) He feels protective because he loves us and wants to help us feel better, just like our moms and dads do. If you could see God when you're scared, what do you think he would do to help you feel better? (*Let kids respond.*) He would hold you close until your fear went away, just like your parents do. God really is with us all the time, and he'll help us conquer our fear if we ask for his help. Praying to God is a good thing to do when we're afraid. God always hears and cares about what we have to say.

Another thing I like to do when I'm afraid is try to remember Scripture verses I've learned. There are lots of verses that can give comfort and courage. For instance, Psalm 56:11 says, "In God I trust; I will not be afraid." When I say a verse like that, I feel brave. What can you do to remember a verse? (*Let kids respond.*) Sometimes I say the verse over and over to help me remember it. When I say verses like Psalm 56:11 over and over, I get braver each time I say it. We should trust God all the time, not just when we're scared. Then when we are scared, it's only natural to remember to trust in God.

Let's say our Scripture verse together before you go back to your seats. I'll say it first to refresh your memories. (*Say the verse including the Scripture reference.*) OK, now it's your turn. Let's say it quietly the first time, like we're scared. (*Say the verse and reference.*) Now let's say it a little louder like we're getting braver. (*Say the verse and reference.*) Sounds like you're gaining courage from God's Word. This will be the last time and I want us to shout the verse like we are the champions over our fear! Ready? (*Shout the verse and reference.*) Do you really trust God? (*Let kids respond.*) That's wonderful! God is always worthy of our trust and love. He will always be there for us.

INTERACTION OPTIONS
Medium: *Have only one person from the congregation share a fear.*
   Low: *Omit congregational involvement in sharing fears.*

In God I trust; I will not be afraid.

God to the Rescue!

THEME: Answered prayer

SCRIPTURE: "He sends from heaven and saves me, rebuking those who hotly pursue me; God sends his love and his faithfulness" (Psalm 57:3).

SUPPLIES NEEDED: A big cushy chair and a pillow, and a cold beverage to sip on.

INTERACTION: *Two men to carry the chair in for you and some women to bring the pillow and cold drink to you.*

(You move gingerly, holding your back on your way up to present the children's message. Say in a pained voice:) Hi, kids! How are you today? *(Let kids respond.)* Well, I'm not so good today. I have a terrible backache. I'm not sure I can sit in my usual spot. *(To helper:)* "Could you please bring me a chair?" *(If you normally sit in a chair during your children's message, ask for a different chair. Helper says "Sure," and leaves to get a chair.)* Boy, I must have slept wrong or something because when I woke up, I had this backache and it just won't go away. I've already taken aspirin for it and it isn't getting any better . . . *(Continue talking about your backache until the men reappear carrying the big cushy chair with the women behind carrying the pillow and drink.)*

(Helper: "Will this be OK? We wanted to be sure you'd be comfortable.") Oh my goodness! That's much nicer than I was expecting! *(Men put the chair up front and women help you get comfortable in it, adjusting the pillow until it's just right and offering you the cool drink.)* Thank you so much! *(Helpers return to their seats.)* Can you believe this, kids? Did you expect them to bring me a chair like this? *(Let kids respond.)* This is even better than I asked for. My back feels better already!

Has anything like this ever happened to you? Have you ever asked for something and got something better than you thought you would get? Tell me about what happened. *(Let kids respond.)* Have you ever asked for something and got less than you thought you would get? What was that like? *(Let kids respond.)* I think that's happened to all of us at one time or another.

Sometimes when I ask God for something, I feel like he doesn't answer my prayers. Why do we feel like God sometimes doesn't answer our prayers? (*Let kids respond.*) Sometimes we don't get what we ask for. But God does answer our prayers even when we don't get what we ask for. His answer may be "no" or "not right now." Other times God may give us an answer that is different than we expect. We might ask God for one thing and he gives us something else instead. In our minds it may be something less than we asked for, or it could be something much better. But the thing to remember is that God knows what's best for us. He always gives us the best thing even if it's not what we had in mind. Our idea of what's best and God's idea of what's best may be different.

For instance, in Psalm 57, wicked King Saul was chasing David. King Saul wanted to kill David. David hid in a cave and prayed to God. What do you think David prayed for? (*Let kids respond.*) David trusted God to save him, but he was still scared. In verse three David said about God. "He sends from heaven and saves me, rebuking those who hotly pursue me; God sends his love and his faithfulness." What did God send to David? (*Let kids respond.*) God didn't make King Saul quit chasing David, but he reassured David of his love and faithfulness. God reminded David that he could trust God to take care of him.

To know the great and mighty creator of the universe is fighting on your side is an awesome feeling. It's like getting a big cushy chair when you expected a folding chair, only better.

INTERACTION OPTIONS

Medium: *Have only two helpers who bring you the big cushy chair. Omit women-helpers with pillow and drink.*

Low: *Have a folding chair up front to sit in. After complaining about your backache, tell the kids you "just had a funny thought. Wouldn't it be funny if I said I had a backache and someone brought a recliner chair up for me to sit in during our children's message? That would be incredible." Then proceed to talk about getting more or less than you expect.*

Make Up Your Mind

THEME: Steadfast faith

SCRIPTURE: "My heart is steadfast, O God, my heart is steadfast; I will sing and make music" (Psalm 57:7).

SUPPLIES NEEDED: None

INTERACTION: *Have a small group of people come into the room late and try to decide where to sit. The people will each have a different opinion of where they should sit. Finally they decide.*

(As you greet the kids, the group of "latecomers" comes into the church and makes a commotion trying to decide where to sit. Each one has a different opinion of where the best seats are and what makes them the best. After a few moments, you intervene.) Would you just make up your minds and then stick with your decision? It doesn't matter where you sit. Just come in and sit down. I'd like to get our children's message started before church is over! *(Group hurriedly sits down.)*

I'm sorry I got a little bit upset with you. Will you forgive me? *(Helpers smile and nod.)* Sometimes I get impatient with people who can't make up their minds. But then again, sometimes I'm the one who can't decide. We all have times when we just can't figure out what we really want. For instance, have you ever heard your parents say, "Close that refrigerator door! You've been standing and looking in there for too long! You'll let all the cool air out!" Why do we stand with the fridge door open? *(Let kids respond.)* That's right, because we can't decide what we want to eat. Or how about this one? This is a great parent (or wife) line. "Stop flipping the channel changer on the remote and choose one show to watch!" Why do we flip channels? *(Let children respond.)* Sometimes I can't decide whether to buy apples or oranges at the grocery store. It's silly.

Some decisions in life aren't all that important. But it's important not to be wishy-washy about important decisions like following Jesus. We need to be sure about what we believe before we decide. In Psalm 57:7 David says, "My heart is steadfast, O God, my heart is steadfast; I will sing and make music." What does steadfast mean? *(Let kids respond.)* Steadfast means unchanging. David wasn't going to change his mind about following God because his heart was steadfast.

He'd made up his mind and he was going to stick to his decision no matter what. It's good to have a steadfast heart when it comes to loving God. When it comes to little decisions like where to sit in church *(motion toward helpers)*, or what we get out of the fridge, it doesn't really matter what we decide. But when you decide to follow Jesus, it's important that you stick to your decision with a steadfast heart.

INTERACTION OPTIONS

Medium: *One person to keep changing his or her mind about whether or not to join the kids for the children's message.*

Low: *Begin by asking kids if they've ever had trouble making up their minds about something. What was it? Then proceed with second paragraph.*

My heart is steadfast, O God, . . . I will sing and make music.

Follow the Leader

THEME: Praying for our leaders

SCRIPTURE: "Increase the days of the king's life, his years for many generations. May he be enthroned in God's presence forever; appoint your love and faithfulness to protect him" (Psalm 61:6, 7).

SUPPLIES NEEDED: Slips of paper, each with the name of a leader and suggestions for prayer, one for each child.

INTERACTION: *Ask all the people in the congregation who are currently in positions of leadership to stand. Their positions of leadership could be in their job, their family, their community, their church, etc. Show kids how many leaders there are and how many people just in your own church need prayer. You may want to have some of these people's names on the slips of paper you give to the kids. Or make the slips after the people stand so you know what names to use.*

Hi, kids! It's great to see you. Would you like to play a game with me today? Let's play Follow the Leader. Just to refresh your memory, the way we play is I will do something like skip or hop, and you do whatever I do. Ready? (*Lead the kids in a short game of Follow the Leader.*) That was fun!

You kids did a great job of following. In our game we had a leader. There are lots of different leaders in our world. What are some other types of leaders? (*Let kids respond.*) What do leaders do? (*Let kids respond.*) There are leaders of countries, churches, companies, hikes, Boy Scout and Girl Scout troops, classrooms, and many other groups. We have many leaders in our church. I would like all the leaders in our congregation to please stand. You may be a leader in your job, your family, community, church, or something else. But if you're a leader in some capacity, please stand. (*Pause a moment while people stand.*) That's a lot of leaders!

Thank you for your leadership. Let's give them all a big hand. (*Applause.*) You may be seated.

Leaders have a lot of responsibilities. They're in charge of keeping things running smoothly and safely for everyone. That can be a big job. Have any of you ever been a leader in something? (*Let kids tell about their leadership experiences.*)

Because leaders have so much responsibility, we need to pray for them. Even if we don't agree with all the things they do, we still need to pray for them so they will make good decisions. In Bible times when David lived, the leader of his country was a king. In Psalm 61:6, 7, David prayed for the king. He said, "Increase the days of the king's life, his years for many generations. May he be enthroned in God's presence forever; appoint your love and faithfulness to protect him." David prayed for the king to have a long life, protected by God's love and faithfulness.

What are some things we can pray for our leaders? (*Let kids respond.*) It's good to pray for their safety, for their health, and for the decisions they make. We can pray they will look to God and the Bible for advice in making decisions, and that they will be the kind of people who please God. We could pray for them not to be tempted to do wrong, but to take a strong stand for what's right. These are the kind of prayers we can pray for our leaders and for anyone we care about. Children grow up to be leaders and we need to pray for them too, so they will grow up to be good leaders who God will be proud of.

Before we go back to our seats, I'm going to give you each an assignment. I need you to promise to pray for someone all week long. I have slips of paper here with the name of a leader on each one and suggestions of things you can pray for. (*Hand a slip of paper to each child.*) You've all just received a very important assignment. These people need your help. They need your prayers. So remember to pray for your assigned leader and any others you may want to pray for also. It's one way we can make the world a better place.

INTERACTION OPTIONS

Medium: *Have a volunteer lead the game of Follow the Leader. Omit the portion where leaders in the congregation stand.*

Low: *Lead the game of Follow the Leader yourself. Or let one of the kids be the leader.*

That's My Dad!

THEME: God as Father

SCRIPTURE: "A father to the fatherless, a defender of widows, is God in his holy dwelling" (Psalm 68:5).

SUPPLIES NEEDED: None

INTERACTION: *Fathers in the congregation share a proud memory of their children.*

Good morning! How are you today? (*A father in the congregation stands and says, "Excuse me, but could I tell you about something I'm really proud of?"*) Sure. Go ahead. (*Father shares a story of a time he felt proud of his child.*) Wow—that's really neat! Thanks for sharing that with us. (*Another father stands and says, "Yeah, I know what you mean. I remember a time when . . ." and goes on to tell a story about when he was proud of his child.*) Well, that's wonderful. I'm glad you have such proud moments to share with us. But we really need to get to our children's message. (*Another father stands and says, "I understand, but this is just too good to keep to myself. I just have to tell you about the time my child . . ." and the father tells a story of when he was proud of his child.*) OK, thank you. I'm sorry but we really don't have time for any more stories. I know you're all very proud of your children. They're all such wonderful kids.

Kids, your dads are sure proud of you. They love you very much, don't they? But unfortunately, not all kids have a dad. There are lots of different kinds of families. Some families have a mom and a dad. Some have only a dad or a mom. Some have neither a dad nor a mom, but the kids live with their grandparents or someone else. Lots of kids live in families where the mom and dad are divorced and they live part of the time with their mom and part of the time with their dad. What kind of family do you have? (*Let kids respond.*) There are so many different kinds of families that I can't even list them all.

I know that when kids live with their moms they sometimes feel sad because they miss their dads. Or maybe their dad died and they wish he'd come back even though they know he can't. In Psalm 68:5 there is a wonderful promise for children who miss their dads. It's also a promise for their moms to hold onto. The promise is that God will be "a father to the fatherless, a defender of widows." What do you think David meant when he said "a father to the fatherless"? (*Let kids respond.*) God is a father to everyone—even people who don't have a dad.

God is a father to all of us. He's the perfect father. He never makes a mistake, he always has time for us, and he's never out of town! And when we feel alone, God is always there. He loves us even when we mess up, and he gives us the strength and wisdom to do better the next time. Our dads here on earth do the best they can, but they're only human. They can't be perfect. So be thankful if you have a dad on earth. Let him know you love and appreciate him. And the next time you or a friend need a dad to talk to and an earthly dad isn't around, talk to God, your heavenly Dad. He loves you and is proud of you just like the dads in our congregation are proud of their kids.

INTERACTION OPTIONS

Medium: *Have only one dad share a proud moment about his child.*

Low: *Omit paragraph one. Begin message by talking about different types of families. Ask kids what kinds of families they have.*

A father to the fatherless, a defender of widows, is God.

Never Alone

THEME: Loneliness

SCRIPTURE: "God sets the lonely in families" (Psalm 68:6).

SUPPLIES NEEDED: None

INTERACTION: *Have a group of people (could be a Sunday school class or Bible study group) come up and say they're feeling sad because one of their friends is moving away.*

(As you invite the kids to come up, your helpers trudge up with them.) Well hello. It's good to see you, but I must admit I'm surprised to see you all come up with the kids today. *(Helpers nod and maintain their gloomy dispositions.)* You don't seem to be your usual chipper selves today. Is something wrong? *(Helpers nod.)* Would you like to tell us about it? Sometimes it helps to share your problems with people who care about you. *(Spokesperson for the group: "Well, OK. A good friend in our Sunday school class is moving away and we would like to throw her a going away party, but we just feel too sad to party. We're going to miss her so much! I don't know what we'll do without her.)*

I'm sorry you're feeling sad and lonely. It's hard to lose someone you love. *(To kids:)* Have any of you ever felt that way? What was that like? *(Let kids respond.)* Boy, loneliness can sure make you feel sad. Even when you're with people, you can still feel lonely if you're not with someone you care about. Sometimes we feel lonely even when we're with our families, like when our best friend moves away. What can we do when we're lonely? *(Let kids respond.)* Did you know we have a second family to help us feel better? It's called the family of God, and it's made up of every Christian on earth. Did you know that you have family members in cities and countries you've never even been to? Because Christians all love God, we have a special kind of love for each other that no one else can share or understand. So when one person feels sad and lonely, we all care and want to help.

Psalm 68:6 says, "God sets the lonely in families." God knows that the best place for someone feeling lonely is with his family. But our own family may not always understand or have time to listen. So when that happens, go to your second family for help. Your family of God is bigger than your own family and there is probably someone who has been through the same thing you may be struggling with and will understand how you feel. So don't forget to reach out to your own family and your family of God when you need someone to help you, pray for you, or listen to you. Loneliness can be a hard thing to work through, and it's easier when you have your family by your side.

(*Spokesperson says, "It's great to have a second family! We'll really miss our friend, but at least we still have our Christian family to help us get through the loneliness."*)

INTERACTION OPTIONS

Medium: *Someone to act discouraged and lonely because his or her best friend moved away.*

Low: *Begin by asking kids if they've ever felt lonely. How did it make them feel?*

God sets the lonely in families.

God's Parade

THEME: Praising God

SCRIPTURE: "Your procession has come into view, O God, . . . In front are the singers, after them the musicians; with them are the maidens playing tambourines. Praise God in the great congregation; praise the Lord in the assembly of Israel" (Psalm 68:24-26).

SUPPLIES NEEDED: Rhythm band instruments such as sticks, tambourines, cymbals (or pan lids to clang together), keys to jingle, anything that can make music! Optional: candy to toss to the congregation.

INTERACTION: *A singer in your congregation who will lead the kids' parade in song. Have the congregation sing along or clap their hands. Optional: Have people (including kids) who play instruments bring them and ask them to join the parade.*

Hi, kids! We're going to have lots of fun today. How many of you have seen a parade? (*Let kids respond.*) What do you see in a parade? (*Let kids respond.*) You see clowns, bands, floats, horses—almost anything can be in a parade.

The Bible tells us about a parade. In Psalm 68:24-26 David talks about a parade for God. He calls it a procession. He says, "Your procession has come into view, O God, the procession of my God and King into the sanctuary. In front are the singers, after them the musicians; with them are the maidens playing tambourines. Praise God in the great congregation; praise the Lord in the assembly of Israel." God's parade sounds a little like the parades we have today. It had singers and people playing musical instruments. They were praising God with their parade. When I read those verses I thought, "Why don't we praise God like that?" Let's have a parade like the parade in the Bible. David tells us that the singers were in front. Because (name) has such a beautiful voice, I've asked him (or her) to lead the singers in our parade.

(Name), will you come up and lead us? Maybe you could sing "Awesome God" (or any familiar song). Who would like to sing with (name)? (If no children volunteer, ask for two or three adult volunteers.) Wonderful!

Next came the musicians; I have a few instruments here that we can use. (Pass out instruments except for the tambourines. If there are more children than instruments, suggest they use their bodies as instruments—clap hands, click tongues, snap fingers.) After that came the maidens playing tambourines. Maidens are girls. Would any of you girls like to play a tambourine? (If not, allow the boys to, saying that our parade can be different from the one in the Bible, and that tambourines aren't just for girls.)

(Optional: Give handfuls of candy to children who didn't get an instrument and let them toss it into the congregation. You could also have some people who play instruments stand and ask if they can join you with their instruments.)

Let's line up. (Pick up your Bible and refer to it.) Singers first, then musicians, then tambourine players. OK (looking at Bible again), now it says to "praise God in the great congregation." I think our congregation is pretty great, don't you? Let's praise God with our parade among this great congregation. Let's have our congregation join us in praise by singing along and clapping their hands.

All right singers, lead the way! (Helper leads the parade with the singers singing "Awesome God" while marching down the aisle. All other parade members follow. You take up the rear, encouraging the congregation to sing and clap. Remind everyone that a parade is a festive occasion. Have the kids come back to starting position and tell them that praising God is so much fun that we are going to have the parade all over again. Helper should end the parade by leading the kids back to where you started.)

That was fun! What part did you enjoy the most? (Let kids respond.) What do you suppose God was thinking while he watched us? (Let kids respond.) I think God loved and accepted our praise. The next time you go to a parade, remember the parade in the Bible and thank God for the fun we can have praising him.

INTERACTION OPTIONS

Medium: Have a singer lead the kids in the parade while they play their rhythm band instruments. Have congregation sing along while kids march.

Low: Have kids play rhythm band instruments for parade. Omit the other participants. Have pianist play "Awesome God" while kids march in parade.

I Need You

THEME: The needy

SCRIPTURE: "The Lord hears the needy and does not despise his captive people" (Psalm 69:33).

SUPPLIES NEEDED: A cardboard sign that reads, "Will work for food."A glass of water, a cookie, a jacket—anything someone can offer to a homeless person.

INTERACTION: *One person to act as a homeless person carrying a cardboard sign. Several helpers to offer the homeless person something (water, cookie, a jacket, a ride some-where, etc.).*

Leader: Good morning! It's good to see you. (*Homeless helper comes walking down the aisle holding his or her "Will work for food" sign.*) "Will work for food"? What's this? Where did you come from?

Homeless helper (*shrugs:*) I come from nowhere. I don't have a home. I don't have a job. No one listens and no one cares.

Leader: I'm sorry to hear that. Would you like to sit down and join us for a moment?

Homeless helper: I guess." (*He sits down.*)

First helper from congregation (*stands and says:*) Would you like a glass of water?

Homeless helper: That sounds delicious. Thank you. (*First helper gives homeless person a glass of water and returns to seat. Second helper offers homeless person a cookie and brings it to him. This continues with all helpers until items are all distributed.*) I guess some people do care. May I stay here and listen?

Leader: Of course you may. (*Ask kids:*) Have you ever felt as if no one cared? What was that like? (*Let kids respond.*) It may sometimes seem as if no one cares, but that doesn't make it true. (*To homeless helper:*) There are many in this room who care about you right now. We want good things for you in your life. If there's some way we can help you, we'd like to try. But you know who cares even more? (*Helper shakes his head.*) God does. Psalm 69:33 says, "The Lord hears the needy and does not despise his captive people." Who do you think he's talking about?

Homeless helper: Me, I guess. I'm about as needy as they come.

Leader: God hears your prayers and he cares. (*To class:*) Kids, do you think people who don't have much money are the only needy people in the world? (*Let kids respond.*) Who else might be needy? (*Let kids give their ideas.*) Everyone needs something. We all need food, water, shelter, clothes, friends, love, and security. We have many needs. Our most important need is to know Jesus. Only he can take care of our deepest needs.

The last part of our verse said that the Lord "does not despise his captive people." What does it mean to be held captive? (*Let kids respond.*) Who are captive people? (*Let kids respond.*) We usually think of people who are in jail as captives, but that phrase could apply to us, too. We may not be held captive in jail, but we're held captive by our sinful lives and our fears. God doesn't hate us because we're prisoners of sin and fear. He loves us. He wants to help us break free. We can make a great escape! How can we do that? (*Let kids respond.*) By accepting Jesus as our Savior and asking him to be with us forever. Then each day he'll be here beside us to keep us free from the temptations, struggles, and fears we face.

God helps the needy, and so can we! How could we help (name of homeless helper)? (*Let kids respond.*) Take a minute right now to think of someone who might be needy. Without saying his or her name, think of someone who is lonely or afraid. Maybe you have a friend in school who has trouble reading or doing math. Tell me one way you could help that friend who is needy. (*Let kids respond.*)

(*To helper:*) Would you read our Scripture verse in Psalm 69:33 for us again? (*To class:*) This time as the verse is read, I want us all to think of ourselves as needy people and captives of sin. (*Helper reads verse.*) We're all needy and we can work together to help each other.

INTERACTION OPTIONS

Medium: *One person to act like a homeless person carrying cardboard sign. Someone else to get him or her a glass of water.*

Low: *Begin by asking kids if they have ever seen a homeless person on the street. Talk about how that person might feel and how God feels toward him or her. Then read the Scripture verse.*

Baby Praise

THEME: Never too young to trust in God

SCRIPTURE: "For you have been my hope, O Sovereign Lord, my confidence since my youth. From birth I have relied on you; you brought me forth from my mother's womb. I will ever praise you" (Psalm 71:5, 6).

SUPPLIES NEEDED: An apple, a sharp knife, a large paintbrush, and a set of car keys.

INTERACTION: *Three of the kids' parents to stand up at the appropriate time and say their kids can't do what you're asking them to do because they're too young.*

Hi, kids. How are you today? (*Let kids respond.*) Good! I'm doing pretty well myself, but I was hoping you would help me with a few things today. First of all, let me explain that I'm one of those crazy people who will eat apples only if they're cut into pieces. Are any of you like that? I really wanted to have an apple for breakfast today, but I didn't have time to cut it. So I brought the apple and the knife with me (*pull knife and apple out of bag*) in hopes that (name one of the younger children) would cut it for me while I give the children's message.

(*Child's parent jumps up and says, "Wait just a minute! I don't want my child to cut that apple for you. He might cut himself. He doesn't use sharp knives yet."*)

Oh. OK, I guess I could cut it and eat it later. Thanks anyway.

The next thing I need help with is some painting. I noticed that there are a few spots on the church walls that are starting to look a little worn. (Name of a young girl), would you do some painting for me? (*Bring out the paintbrush.*) The only problem is that I forgot to bring a drop cloth to put down on the floor to catch any drips or spills.

(*Child's parent jumps up. "Oh no. My daughter isn't going to be responsible for painting the church, especially if there are no drop cloths. She isn't quite old enough yet."*)
Hmm. OK, if you say so. Sorry, (name). Maybe another time when you're older.

(*To one of the older kids:*) Would you help me with something? I parked my car in a parking space for the handicapped because I had some things to unload and I wanted to be close to the building to do it. But I haven't had time to go back out to the parking lot and move it to a regular parking space yet. (*Pull out your car keys and jingle them as if to tempt the child.*) Would you move my car for me?

(*Child's parent jumps up. "For crying out loud! Are you nuts? My child can't drive! He's only ___ years old! He doesn't even have a driver's license!"*)

Well, of course not. I'm not asking him to drive in the street. Only in the parking lot. How about it?

(*Parent: "Absolutely not! My child cannot drive in the street or the parking lot or anywhere else until he is older."*)

Oh, OK. Maybe in a few more years. Guess I'll have to move my own car.

Your parents are right. The things I asked you to do were things that older people should do. But do you ever get tired of being too young to do some things you'd like to do? (*Let kids respond.*) What are some things you wish you could do now that you have to wait to do until you're older? (*Let kids respond.*) How old do you have to be before you can do those things? (*Let kids respond.*) How old do you think you have to be before you can trust in God? (*Let kids guess.*) When do you think you're too old to trust in him? (*Let kids guess.*) The amazing thing about trusting God is that you're never too young or too old to do it. As a matter of fact, the writer of Psalm 71:5, 6 talks about when he began to trust or rely on God. Listen closely to see if you hear how old he was. "For you have been my hope, O Sovereign Lord, my confidence since my youth. From birth I have relied on you; you brought me forth from my mother's womb. I will ever praise you." When did this writer begin relying on God? (*Let kids respond.*) When he was born! As long as he can remember, he trusted in God. And when does he plan to quit praising God? (*Let kids respond.*) Never! He said he will ever, or always, praise God.

So the next time you feel like you're too young to do anything important, remember you're never too young—or too old—to trust in God. And there's nothing more important than that!

INTERACTION OPTIONS

Medium: *Ask one child (the younger the better) to do all three situations. His parent will object more strenuously each time.*

Low: *Make believe the situations. For instance, say, "If I were to ask (name of a young child) to cut this apple for me, what do you think his (or her) parents would say?"*

Off of the Lap

THEME: Drawing near to God

SCRIPTURE: "But as for me, it is good to be near God. I have made the Sovereign Lord my refuge; I will tell of all your deeds" (Psalm 73:28).

SUPPLIES NEEDED: None

INTERACTION: *The parent of grown children will act sad because his/her children don't need him/her anymore. The grown child (or someone to act as the child) will respond to helper's claim that s/he is no longer needed.*

Come on up, kids. Let's have our children's message. (*Helper gets up and trudges down to you also.*) Well, hello. You look a little down. What's the matter? (*Helper explains that his/her kids are all grown up now and don't need him/her anymore. Grown child stands and says, "That's not true! We just need you in a different way, that's all."* Kids, how do (name)'s children still need him/her? (*Let kids respond.*) They need you to be supportive as they start living their own lives. They'll always need your love, and they'll need a listening ear from time to time. I'll tell you what, why don't you go sit down and we'll talk about this later? The children are waiting patiently for their message right now. (*Helper and grown child say OK and go back to their seats.*)

Someday you'll be all grown up and you'll live in your own houses just like our helper's children do. But growing up happens a little at a time. What things did you do when you were younger that you may not do now? (*Let kids respond.*) When you were younger, you probably liked to sit on your mom and dad's laps a lot of the time. Do you like to do that a lot now? Why or why not? (*Let kids respond.*) As you grow older, that becomes something you do in special moments because usually, you'd rather be playing. How would you feel if your parents always carried you around like a baby and wouldn't let you play? (*Let kids respond.*)

Here's another example: When you go to school, your mom and dad can't go with you. Even if you think you want them to at first, you soon find out it's not as much fun as making your own place in the world without them. You'd miss out on making new friends if you stayed with your mom and dad all the time. You wouldn't learn the games other kids play, or the kinds of jokes they tell.

But still, there are some times it's very reassuring to have your parents near. When do you like to be close to your parents? (*Let kids respond.*) When you're scared or sick. When you want to read books together. When you have something to tell them. It's good to be near your parents.

In the Bible, Asaph the psalmist talks about being near to God. In Psalm 73:28 he says, "But as for me, it is good to be near God. I have made the Sovereign Lord my refuge; I will tell of all your deeds." Asaph was already grown up when he said that. But he knew he still needed to be near God even as a grown-up man, just like you know it's good to be near your parents sometimes. Asaph said he made God his refuge. What is a refuge? (*Let kids respond.*) A refuge is a safe place. God can be a safe place for all of us. What do you think you have to do to make God your refuge? (*Let kids respond.*) You have to trust him and pray to him and let him into your life.

Even though your parents can't be with you all the time, remember God can go with you anywhere.

INTERACTION OPTIONS

Medium: *The parent of grown children to act sad because his/her children don't need him/her anymore. Presenter will respond rather than grown child.*

Low: *Begin by asking the kids what they would like to be when they grow up. Ask them if they're ready to start that job today. Why not? Because they have to learn more about it, go to school, and get older first. Proceed with second paragraph, talking about how growing up happens a little at a time.*

But as for me, it is good to be near God.

Strike Up the Band

THEME: Praising God with music

SCRIPTURE: "Sing for joy to God our strength; shout aloud to the God of Jacob! Begin the music, strike the tambourine, play the melodious harp and lyre" (Psalm 81:1, 2).

SUPPLIES NEEDED: Rhythm band instruments (sticks to click together, wood blocks to hit or rub together, pan lids to clang as cymbals, etc.)

INTERACTION: *The church pianist or organist to talk about when he/she started playing the piano. S/he will accompany the rhythm band. Congregation will join in the fun by singing, whistling, snapping their fingers, jingling their keys, or clapping along to the music.*

Do any of you kids play a musical instrument? (*Let kids respond and tell about any instruments they may play.*) Do you think it's hard to play an instrument? Why or why not? (*Let kids respond.*) It takes lots of practice to be really good at it. Just think of all the years our piano player must have practiced. (*To pianist:*) How many years have you been playing the piano? (*Let pianist respond.*) Wow! That's a lot of years of practicing. You must have been little when you started. (*Pianist tells how old s/he was when s/he first started taking piano lessons.*) Do you still have to practice? (*Pianist responds.*) Would you play a song for us? (*Pianist plays a well-known tune.*) Well, thank you for sharing with us. I'm glad you praise God with your music. We appreciate your piano playing in our service. Let's give our pianist a hand for all his/her hard work. (*Give the pianist a round of applause.*)

Some instruments, like the piano, take a lot of practice. But some don't, like the ones I have here with me. We're going to praise God with music today. What does it mean to praise God? (*Let children respond.*) How can we do that? (*Let children give their ideas.*) God loves to hear our praise. As a matter of fact, praising

God with music isn't a new idea. The people in the Bible were great at praising God with instruments. The author of Psalm 81:1, 2 says, "Sing for joy to God our strength; shout aloud to the God of Jacob! Begin the music, strike the tambourine, play the melodious harp and lyre." We may not have the same instruments he wrote about, but we do have our voices to "sing for joy to God," and we have other instruments we can use. (*Begin handing out instruments.*) The instruments aren't what's important. It's praising God that's important. Are you ready to do that? (*Let kids respond.*) Let's play our instruments while we sing "If You're Happy and You Know It" (*or some other song the kids in your church know*). Maybe our pianist would like to play the piano with us while we sing. (*Pianist gives an affirmative nod or thumbs up.*) And let's have our congregation join us in singing, whistling, snapping your fingers, jingling your keys, or any other way you'd like to praise God musically. Is everyone ready? Let's joyfully praise God! (*Sing song and play instruments.*)

That was wonderful! You really put your whole hearts into praising God. How do you think that made God feel? (*Let kids respond.*) God loves to hear our praises. There's nothing more satisfying than loving God and letting him know it by praising him. You can praise God when you're all by yourself or when you're with your friends. You can praise God anytime, anywhere. There's no right or wrong way to do it. As long as you're thinking good thoughts about God, you're praising him. So let's please God by praising him often.

INTERACTION OPTIONS

Medium: *The church pianist or organist will talk about when he/she started playing the piano or organ. Omit congregational involvement in praise song.*

Low: *Omit the interview with the pianist. Ask the kids if any of them play an instrument. Talk about the amount of practice involved. Proceed with paragraph two.*

Begin the music, strike the tambourine, play the melodious harp and lyre.

I'd Rather Be . . .

THEME: The importance of serving God

SCRIPTURE: "I would rather be a doorkeeper in the house of my God than dwell in the tents of the wicked" (Psalm 84:10).

SUPPLIES NEEDED: None. Optional: "I'd rather be . . ." bumper sticker(s)

INTERACTION: *Two or three people planted in the congregation will say what their "I'd rather be" bumper stickers would (or do!) say.*

Have you ever seen those bumper stickers that say "I'd rather be fishing" or "I'd rather be shopping"? Those bumper stickers tell you a lot about what the person driving that car likes to do. If you could make up your own bumper sticker that said, "I'd rather be . . ." and then fill in one of your favorite activities, what would it say? *(Give kids a moment to think about it and respond.)* Those are great ideas. They sound like a lot of fun. What about some of the people in our congregation? Do any of you have an "I'd rather be . . ." bumper sticker? What does it say? Or if you made up your own bumper sticker, what would it say? *(Let "planted" people in the congregation stand and tell what their bumper sticker would say.)*

Did you know the Bible has an "I'd rather be . . ." bumper sticker in it? Well, OK, it may not have been put on a bumper sticker back in Bible times, but it could be made into a bumper sticker today. The author of Psalm 84:10 says, "I'd rather be a doorkeeper in the house of my God than dwell in the tents of the wicked." Are you surprised? *(Let kids respond.)* I bet you thought I was teasing you!

What do you think this author meant when he wrote those words? *(Repeat the verse and let kids respond.)* What do you think a doorkeeper does? *(Let kids respond.)* A doorkeeper is someone who is in charge of guarding and opening the door for people. Back in Bible times it was one of the most unimportant jobs a person could have. The people who lived inside the house were way more important than the doorkeeper was. The doorkeeper was just a servant to them. David said he'd rather be doing something very unimportant, even be a servant, in God's house than to be one of the important people living inside someone else's house. Why do you think he would say that? *(Let kids respond.)* The most important job a person can do is to serve God. Even if the job looks unimportant to others, if it's done for God, it becomes very important and it makes you feel proud to do it.

How can you serve God? *(Let kids respond. Some ways would be to encourage others, be a friend to others, invite friends to church, share, be kind.)* Those are very important things that make people feel good. Those things let others see Jesus through you and help them to feel God's love for them. If you ever think the ways you serve God aren't important, remember the Bible bumper sticker, "I'd rather be a doorkeeper in the house of my God than dwell in the tents of the wicked." If you're serving God, you are very important.

INTERACTION OPTIONS

Medium: *Have only one person from the congregation stand and tell what his or her "I'd rather be . . ." bumper sticker would (or does) say.*

Low: *Ask the kids what their bumper stickers would say. Omit congregation involvement.*

I would rather be a doorkeeper in the house of my God than dwell in the tents of the wicked.

He Loves Me . . . He Loves Me Not

THEME: Choosing good friends

SCRIPTURE: "Men of perverse heart shall be far from me; I will have nothing to do with evil" (Psalm 101:4).

SUPPLIES NEEDED: A red construction paper heart

INTERACTION: *Several friends in your congregation will share why they like each other.*

Who's one of your best friends? (*Let kids respond.*) Why do you like that person so much? (*Let kids tell about their friend.*) I thought it might be fun to hear from some friends in our congregation and find out what they like about each other. What makes people friends? (*Friends you've preselected in your congregation stand and share why they like each other so much and what makes their friendship special.*) Thank you for sharing your friendships with us. It's great to know there are such good friendships in our congregation.

What do you think of when you hear the word "friend"? (*Let kids respond. They'll probably begin saying words that describe friends. If not, ask them what good friends are like.*) A good friend is kind, fun, helpful, loyal, good at keeping your secrets, and encourages you to do what's right even when it's hard. Good friends have good hearts and aren't ashamed to show them by being kind and loving to others. (*Bring out red construction paper heart.*) Oh, they may make a mistake once in a while, but they still have kind hearts. They want what's best for you. They're happy when something wonderful happens to you, and sad when something bad happens.

Have you ever had someone act like he was your friend, but later you found out he wasn't a very good friend after all? (*Let kids respond.*) How did it make you feel? (*Let kids respond.*) It hurt you, didn't it? (*Hold up heart.*) When you find out a friend isn't really a friend after all, it does this to your heart. (*Tear off a piece of the paper heart.*) It sometimes feels like a piece of your heart has broken right off.

How can you tell when someone isn't a good choice for a friend? (*Let kids respond.*) If he isn't kind to others, he may not be kind to you either. She may say nice things to you when you're around, but say bad things when you're gone. (*Tear another piece of the paper heart off.*) He may not be trustworthy. She may get herself—and you—into trouble by the way she behaves. It's better to stay away from people like that because if you hang around them for very long, you may begin to act like them and be tempted to do the same bad things that they do.

In Psalm 101:4 David says, "Men of perverse heart shall be far from me; I will have nothing to do with evil." Perverse hearts are unkind hearts. People who have unkind hearts often make bad choices. Why should we be very careful around people with unkind hearts? (*Let kids respond.*) Because they are dangerous. Our hearts can be hurt or even broken very easily. (*Tear another piece of the heart off.*) They can be stained with sin (*tear another piece off*), and they can be fooled into thinking bad things are good (*tear another piece of the heart off*). In order to protect our hearts and lives, we need to choose our friends wisely and be very careful around people who do evil and those who have bad hearts. We can love them, but choose not to become like them. God loves them, but he wishes they would be kind and make better choices. We can pray for them to become the kind of people God wants them to be.

So be like David in our Bibles. Protect yourself by choosing good friends and praying for those who do evil.

INTERACTION OPTIONS

Medium: *Ask only one set of friends from the congregation to share about their friendship.*

Low: *Ask kids who one of their best friends is and why they like that person so much. Skip to second paragraph.*

I will have nothing to do with evil.

Moody Moe

THEME: God is unchanging

SCRIPTURE: "But you remain the same, and your years will never end" (Psalm 102:27).

SUPPLIES NEEDED: Moe's cowboy costume. Mother's costume. A bucket for carrying water, a notepad, and pen.

INTERACTION: *Someone to play the parts of the narrator, Moody Moe, and his mother.*

How many of you know the story of Moody Moe? (*Let kids respond.*) Well, I have some friends who are going to act it out for you today.

Narrator: Once there was a boy named Moe. (*Enter Moe wearing cowboy hat.*) He lived in the wild west back in cowboy days. Moe was a happy boy who loved to play. (*Moe pretends to lasso a steer, and swaggers around like a cowboy.*) He spent most of his days running and jumping and pretending to be a cowboy. But as with most families, Moe had some chores he was supposed to do each day. He was supposed to gather wood for the fire, set the table for dinner, and bring his mother water from the creek. One day Moe was in the middle of an imaginary rodeo when his mother came to him carrying a bucket.

Mother (*enters with a water bucket:*) Moe, will you please go to the creek and get me some water? I need it to wash the dishes. And don't forget to gather wood for the fire today. (*Shaking her finger:*) I had to remind you three times yesterday! (*Mother exits, leaving water bucket for Moe.*)

Narrator: Moe didn't feel happy anymore. He felt mad.

Moe (*angry face, hands on his hips:*) Mom always spoils all my fun! (*Angrily grabs bucket and stomps offstage.*)

Narrator: Moe was in a bad mood. This wasn't anything new. He got in a bad mood every day when his mother asked for help. But later, when his chores were done, Moe would be happy again. It seemed to those around him that one minute Moe was happy, the next minute he was mad, and then he'd be happy again for practically no reason at all. Moe's mood changed so quickly that people started calling him "Moody Moe." You can just imagine how Moe liked that.

Moe (*entering angrily:*) I am not moody! (*Exits angrily.*)

Narrator: One day Moe's mother decided she'd write down every time Moe's mood changed. (*Enter Moe's mother with a notepad and pen. She writes as she walks across the stage shaking her head and tsk, tsking.*) She filled a whole page with short notes of Moe's moods and why he was in that mood. Then at the end of the day, she sat down with Moe and showed him the list.

(*Enter Moe and Mother. They sit, and Mother puts her arm around Moe.*)

Mother: Moe, I love you and I want you to have friends and a happy life. That's why I want to try to help you see how moody you are. Look at this list of the times you've been angry in just one day.

Narrator: This time Moe listened. As he read the list, he was shocked.

Moe: I can't believe I've been so moody! I'm sorry, Mom. I'll try to do better.

Mother: You know, Moe, God is willing to help you change. Will you pray with me to ask God to help you think before you speak and act?

Moe: Yes, Mother, I will. I don't want to be so moody. I want to change.

Narrator: And with God's help, he did. The end. (*Lead the applause.*)

It's not bad to feel many different emotions, but it is bad to change from one emotion to the next for no good reason. For example, it's silly to get angry just because your mother asks you for help. I know someone who is never moody like Moe. He's always patient, loving, kind, and forgiving. Sometimes he gets angry, but when he is angry, it's always for a good reason. Do you know who I'm talking about? (*Let kids respond.*) It's God.

The author of Psalm 102:27 says, "You remain the same, and your years will never end." God never changes. He is always faithful to us, he always loves us and he always forgives us when we tell him we're sorry for our sins. We don't have to wonder about what kind of mood God is in when we pray because God is always the same, yesterday, today and forever.

INTERACTION OPTIONS

Medium: *Tell the story while two people pantomime it.*

Low: *Read or tell the story without having it acted out.*

God's Clothes

THEME: God's splendor and majesty

SCRIPTURE: "Praise the Lord, O my soul. O Lord my God, you are very great; you are clothed with splendor and majesty" (Psalm 104:1).

SUPPLIES NEEDED: A variety of costumes that tell something about what kind of job a person has, i.e., a construction worker with a hard hat and tools hanging on his belt; a cook with an apron, a chef's hat, and flour on his or her hands; an athlete in shorts, sweatbands, running shoes; any occupational uniforms; a band uniform; a doctor or nurse; etc. Optional: music to play as the models walk down the runway.

INTERACTION: *As many helpers as you have costumes to put on a fashion show for the kids.*

Have you and your friends ever pretended to be someone else? (*Let kids respond.*) Who did you pretend to be? (*Let kids respond.*) How did your friends know you were being someone else? (*Let kids respond.*) Sometimes it's fun to dress up and see if others can guess who you are. In fact, I have some friends who are going to play that game with us today. They're going to put on a fashion show for us and we're going to see if we can guess who they are or what they do just by what they're wearing.

Would our first model please come down the runway? (*Begin runway music. First helper enters and walks down the aisle, making an occasional spin to show her outfit. Comes to a stop at the front of the church, still making an occasional spin while kids try to guess what she is. Fade out runway music.*) All right, kids. You've seen our first model. What do you think she is (or does)? (*Kids guess.*) How did you know that? (*Kids respond, probably describing her outfit or props.*) Isn't that amazing that we can tell so much about someone by what he or she is wearing?

Thank you, Model #1. (*First model exits down side aisle or out a back door.*) Let's have our second model enter please. (*Repeat as with first model. Have children guess who or what model is. Continue with all other models in same way.*)

Thank you, models, for that beautiful fashion show. Wasn't that fun, kids? Which job would you like to do someday? (*Let kids respond.*)

What kind of clothes do you think God wears? (*Let kids respond.*) Psalm 104:1 says, "Praise the Lord, O my soul. O Lord my God, you are very great; you are clothed with splendor and majesty." Splendor and majesty. What are splendor and majesty? (*Let kids respond.*) That's not exactly the same as wearing a shirt and pants, is it? How could you wear splendor and majesty? (*Let kids respond.*) God is so great his clothes don't even matter. If you could see God, all you would notice would be his greatness, his splendor and majesty. Everything else would become unimportant compared to how awesome God is. The Bible tells us if we looked at God's face we would die because he's so holy and glorious. It would be hard to even notice his clothes. Just like our models' clothes told us who they were, God's clothes of splendor and majesty would show us that he is God. They would remind us how great and wonderful God is.

INTERACTION OPTIONS

Medium: *Have a helper bring a bag of clothes up for the kids to try on one at a time. Kids try to guess what the other children are dressed as.*

Low: *Show the kids pictures of people dressed in different outfits and see if they can guess what their occupation is by what they're wearing.*

Praise the Lord, O my soul. O Lord my God, you are very great.

Do Right

THEME: Doing what's right

SCRIPTURE: "Blessed are they who maintain justice, who constantly do what is right" (Psalm 106:3).

SUPPLIES NEEDED: A toy

INTERACTION: *Six helpers to act out three different situations—two per scene.*

Today we're going to watch some adults act out some situations and I want you to decide whether they did the right thing in each one by giving them a thumb-up or thumbs-down signal.

(Helpers act out a short scene where one child leaves a toy on the playground and the other child takes it and insists it was his.)

Thank you, (names of helpers). *(Helpers return to their seats.)* What do you think, kids? Thumbs-up or thumbs-down? *(Let kids respond.)* Why did you vote that way? *(Let kids respond.)* Was it right for that person to take the toy and say it was his? *(Let kids respond.)* Why? *(Let kids respond.)*

Let's see another situation. *(Second pair of helpers act out scene of parent asking child to clean his/her room. Parent leaves the stage, and child continues playing instead of cleaning his/her room.)*

Thank you, (names of helpers). *(Helpers return to their seats.)* Thumbs-up or thumbs-down, kids? *(Let kids respond.)* Why? *(Let kids respond.)* When our parents ask us to do something, we should obey.

Let's see one more situation. *(Last pair of helpers act out a scene of two kids playing. One child accidentally breaks the other's toy, though the other child doesn't know it. First child tells second child he broke his toy and apologizes.)*

Thumbs-up or thumbs-down? *(Let kids respond.)* Why? *(Let kids respond.)* It's good to be honest with people, even when it's hard. It's the right thing to do.

God wants us to always choose to do right even when it's hard. Psalm 106:3 says, "Blessed are they who maintain justice, who constantly do what is right."

How often is constantly? (*Let kids respond.*) It's all the time, isn't it? Blessed is another word for happy, but what is justice? (*Let kids respond.*) Justice is being fair and honest. So our verse says "happy are the people who are fair and those who always do what's right." Do you think it's hard or easy to always do what's right? (*Let kids respond.*) Why? (*Let kids respond.*) Even though it may be hard, trying to always make the right choices leads to a better life. You'll have fewer problems, fewer fights, and less stress.

How do we know what the right choices are? (*Let kids respond.*) That's right, by reading our Bibles. It's our life's instruction manual. So when you're faced with decisions, try to do right, even if it's hard.

INTERACTION OPTIONS

Medium: *Have the same two people act out all three situations.*

Low: *Instead of having situations acted out, give the kids situations to think about such as "Your friend has a toy you really like. When he leaves it laying on the playground one day, you take it and say it's yours."*

Blessed are they who maintain justice, who constantly do what is right.

Rain, Rain Go Away

THEME: God's peace

SCRIPTURE: "He stilled the storm to a whisper; the waves of the sea were hushed" (Psalm 107:29).

SUPPLIES NEEDED: A spill-proof container half full of dry beans, rice, buttons, or anything else that will make hail-like noise when its shaken. A piece of poster board or sheet metal to shake for the sound of thunder.

INTERACTION: *Someone to lead the children in making storm sounds by using their bodies. Invite the congregation to join you in making the storm sounds.*

How many of you like thunder and lightning cracking the sky and the wind blowing and rain pounding loudly on the roof? (*Let kids raise their hands.*) Then sometimes it starts to hail and that's even louder. How many of you like really bad storms? (*Let children raise their hands.*) Why or why not? (*Let children respond.*) Maybe if we made our own storm that we could control and stop whenever we wanted, it wouldn't be so scary. I have a friend who can teach us how to make a storm by just using our bodies and a few other items. (*Helper comes up.*)

Helper: Let's each make a noise like wind by blowing through our mouths. (*Let them try.*) Sounds like it's getting windy in here. Good job. Let's keep that wind going while we gently pat our hands on our legs to make the rain begin to softly fall. (*Wait a moment while children make rain sound softly on their legs. Wind and rain continue while you talk.*) Sounds like a soft spring shower is beginning. But now the rain is starting to come down harder (*pat legs harder*) and harder (*pat legs even harder to make more noise*). This is no spring shower. This is a downpour! There's the sound of thunder rumbling overhead (*shake the poster board or metal*). The wind is really picking up (*make wind noise louder*). Guess what's coming next? The hail! (*You pull out the container of beans and shake it to make hail noise. If your group is small, you can pass the thunder and hail-makers around to the children to let* *them take turns.)* This is quite a storm! *(Take a moment to listen to the storm. Then in a soothing voice:)* But now it's beginning to pass. The hail has stopped. The thunder is getting farther away. *(Stop shaking the container and sheet. If children have them, quietly take them away.)* The wind is beginning to die down *(quiet your blowing until it's stopped completely)*, and our rain is beginning to get softer and softer *(gradually decrease the speed and volume of rain on your legs)*, until at last, the storm is over and the rain completely stops. *(Stop patting your legs.)* You did a fantastic job making a storm. Give yourselves a hand.

Wow! Thank you, (name)! That was a lot of fun. What wonderful storm makers you are. Was that storm scary? *(Let kids respond.)* Why or why not? *(Let kids respond.)* It's not as scary when it's just a play storm, is it? Sometimes when tough times come into your life it's like a storm. Like when you're sick, or having a hard time at school, or your parents aren't getting along. It's a little scary because you may not know what to do and you may feel like you're getting blown away in the wind and rain. You can't control all of life's situations, just like we can't control a real storm. And that's what makes a storm of life scary, like a bad rainstorm.

But the wonderful thing about belonging to Christ is that we know who can control the storms. God makes the rainstorms. He decides when to make it rain and when to make it stop. He doesn't make the bad situations in our lives happen, but he is still in control of our lives and can help us through the bad times if we let him. God gives us his peace and a calmness we wouldn't have on our own. He can even change the circumstances we're in if he thinks that's the best thing for us. But most often he would rather we learn to trust him instead of changing things around for us so it's easier.

Psalm 107:29 says, "He stilled the storm to a whisper; the waves of the sea were hushed." God is powerful enough that he can actually calm a storm. But often in the storms of life, God chooses to calm us instead. He gives us his peace so we can walk through the storm unafraid.

INTERACTION OPTIONS

Medium: *Have someone lead the children in making storm sounds, but omit congregational involvement.*

Low: *Lead the kids in the storm yourself.*

My Turn

THEME: Generosity

SCRIPTURE: "Good will come to him who is generous and lends freely, who conducts his affairs with justice" (Psalm 112:5).

SUPPLIES NEEDED: Two cookies, one big and one small

INTERACTION: *Two people to act out a scene of one person offering the other a cookie, even though there are not enough to go around. A few people in the congregation to urge the one helper to go ahead and have a cookie.*

Leader: Hello, kids. How are you today? (*Helpers come up.*)

First helper: Hey, (*name of second helper*), I brought you a surprise!

Second helper: Well, how nice! What is it?

First helper: I brought you a cookie. And I brought me one too, so we could enjoy them together.

Second helper: That's very thoughtful of you. But usually a person doesn't offer someone food in front of others unless there's enough for everyone. You see, there are all these other people here who probably want a cookie too, and there aren't enough to go around.

First helper: I know, but I really wanted to give it to you now. They won't mind if you have one. They'd understand that there just aren't enough for everyone. (*To congregation and kids:*) Wouldn't you understand? (*The people planted in the congregation encourage second helper to take the cookie, saying they'd understand.*)

Second helper: Well, OK, if you're really sure. I see you have two kinds. Which shall I take?

First helper: Take whichever one you want.

Second helper: OK, I'll take this one. (*Helper takes a bite of the large cookie.*)

First helper: You chose that one? That's the one I wanted!

Second helper: Well, you told me to take whichever one I wanted!

First helper: Yeah, but I didn't think you really would. I was just being polite. I thought you'd take the smaller one. Now I'm stuck with this little bitty cookie. (*First helper walks off pouting. Second helper throws up his hands in exasperation and walks off.*)

Which do you think is more important? Getting the biggest cookie or keeping a good friend? (*Let kids respond.*) Why? (*Let kids respond.*) I would say keeping a good friend, because after you eat your cookie, it's gone. But you can enjoy years of fun with a friend. Some people like to argue over silly things, like who should be first in line, who got a bigger piece of cake, or whose turn it is to sit in the front of the car. But when they argue over things like that, it's like saying those things are more important than their friendship with that person. They'd rather have their friend mad at them than be generous and let the other guy be first, or have the biggest cookie.

How does it feel to be treated unfairly? (*Let kids respond.*) Sometimes things aren't fair. Maybe it really was your turn to sit in the front seat of the car. But God would rather we love each other than fight over silly things like whose turn it was. Is it easy to give in when you think you're right, or when you really want something badly? (*Let kids respond.*) Why? (*Let kids respond.*)

Taking turns is another way of sharing, and sharing is a way of being generous. Tell me about a time you shared or maybe even a time when you found it hard to share. (*Let kids respond.*) God has a special promise for those who are generous. He knows it takes grown-up behavior to let someone else have something we want. Psalm 112:5 says, "Good will come to him who is generous and lends freely, who conducts his affairs with justice." If you're generous, not selfish, God promises that good will come to you. The Bible also tells us that good will come if you handle things fairly and honestly. What does that mean? (*Let kids respond.*) That means if it isn't your turn in the front seat, you shouldn't say it is. Or if you got to go first in a game last time, then let someone else go first this time. Go ahead and be generous and fair. God always keeps his promises, and he's waiting to bless you.

INTERACTION OPTIONS

Medium: *Omit the part where people in the congregation urge second helper to have a cookie.*

Low: *Tell a situation, rather than act it out, about a friend who offered you a cookie, but then got mad when you took the one he or she wanted.*

My Bodyguard

THEME: Trusting God

SCRIPTURE: "It is better to take refuge in the Lord than to trust in man" (Psalm 118:8).

SUPPLIES NEEDED: None

INTERACTION: *Someone to play the part of a person hiring a body-guard. A big, strong man and a small woman to act as candidates for the job.*

Leader: Hi, kids. It's good to see you. (*Helper comes sneaking in, looking over his shoulder as if someone is following him.*) Hello, (name). What's the matter?

Helper: I think someone is following me and may want to hurt me, so I've decided to hire a bodyguard to protect me.

Leader: A bodyguard?

Helper: You know, someone to keep me safe. I need the kids and you to help me make a decision between two people I've interviewed for the job.

Leader: We don't know much about hiring bodyguards, but we'll be glad to help, won't we kids? (*Let kids respond.*)

Helper: Good. I brought the candidates with me. (*The small female candidate comes up.*) Well, what do you think of this one?

Leader: She's not very big for a bodyguard.

Helper: Maybe not, but she takes ballet classes, so she's really strong. She's a gourmet cook and she loves to sing. She's a great woman with a good heart. She owns a flyswatter and says she'd do about anything to keep me safe.

Leader: Is that it? Those are her qualifications?

Helper (*nodding:*) Sounds pretty good, huh?

Leader: Well, those are fine qualities, but I'm not sure if they fit the profile of a bodyguard. Let's hear about the other candidate. (*Big, strong male walks in.*)

Helper: He has a black belt in karate, has been a bodybuilder for ten years, and is known as an honest man who works hard. Oh, and he's been a bodyguard for several other people in the past five years, all of whom are still living.

Leader *(to candidates:)* Would you mind giving us a little privacy while we talk about this?

(Candidates say "sure" and exit.) What do you think, kids? Who would make the better bodyguard for our friend? *(Let the kids respond.)* Why? *(Let kids respond.)* Without a doubt, the second candidate sounds like he's more qualified for the job. I'm sure the woman is a good person, but I don't think you should trust your life to her. If you were faced with real danger, she might not be able to handle it.

Helper: All right. I think I'll hire the guy. Thanks for your help. *(He slinks off, keeping a low profile.)*

That was interesting. It makes me think of someone else we can trust with our lives. Not only our lives, but also our problems, our worries, our joys, and our sorrows. Do you know who I'm talking about? *(Let kids respond.)* It's God. Why can you trust God? *(Let kids respond.)* It's good to have friends and family to talk things over with when we have something on our minds. But they aren't perfect, and may not always give perfect advice. People may disappoint us. They may not be available when we need them. They may have problems of their own that make it hard for them to listen to our problems.

The choice is as clear as hiring the best bodyguard for our friend. We can choose weak, sinful humans to place our trust in, or the all-powerful God, creator of the universe. The only one we can trust completely is God. God is always available, gives perfect advice in the Bible, and will never disappoint us like people can. Psalm 118:8 says, "It is better to take refuge in the Lord than to trust in man." A refuge is a safe place. God is our safe place, and he is completely trustworthy. So trust God's advice when making decisions; he'll never let you down.

INTERACTION OPTIONS

Medium: *Have person hiring the bodyguard describe the two candidates instead of bringing them along. (The first one is a girl who is five feet tall and weighs ninety pounds, and the second one is a six foot three man who weighs 250 pounds, for instance.)*

Low: *Pretend you're the one hiring a bodyguard and let the kids help you decide which one to hire.*

Good Day!

THEME: Being thankful for each day

SCRIPTURE: "This is the day the Lord has made; let us rejoice and be glad in it" (Psalm 118:24).

SUPPLIES NEEDED: A flower

INTERACTION: *Three helpers. One to give you a flower, one to compliment you on a character trait, one to invite you out for lunch after church.*

Leader: Good morning, kids! Boy, I'm feeling really good today. How about you? *(Let kids respond.)* That's good.

First helper *(enters with a flower:)* Good morning, (name of leader). I brought you a flower today just because I thought you might enjoy it. Have a nice day!

Leader: Well, isn't that nice? Thank you! *(Helper exits.)* How about that? This was already a good day and then this happens to make it even better.

Second helper *(enters, addressing you by name:)* (Name), I've been meaning to tell you how much I appreciate your thoughtfulness. You do so many kind things for people and I just want you to know I appreciate you. *(Helper pats you on the back and exits.)*

Leader: Man! I can't believe this. What a wonderful day this is.

Third helper *(comes in excitedly:)* (Name), I've been looking for you all over the building! Are you free for lunch today? I'd love to treat you to lunch at the restaurant of your choice; would you like that?

Leader: Treat me to lunch? What a wonderful surprise! Of course, I'd like that! I'll meet you in the parking lot right after church, OK? And thank you very much! *(Helper exits.)* Wow! God has really blessed me today, hasn't he?

Have you ever had a really good day? *(Let kids respond.)* What makes a day good? *(Let kids respond.)* When good things happen it seems like an extra good day. What about when things aren't going so well? Can you have a good day then?

(*Let kids respond.*) When you think about it, even if I hadn't been given this pretty flower, and received that nice compliment, and been invited to lunch, it is still a good day. My friends aren't always so generous, but they are always my friends. Even if I hadn't heard from my friends today, it's still a good day because I'm not sick in bed, the sun is shining, and I have people I love who love me back.

Psalm 118:24 says, "This is the day the Lord has made; let us rejoice and be glad in it." According to this verse, why should we rejoice and be glad for today? (*Let kids respond.*) Was it because everything was going great? (*Let kids respond.*) No. It's because God made the day. With God in our lives, we can enjoy each day. Every day may not go exactly the way we'd like, but it's good to know we are never alone because God is always there to help us through each day, whether it is a good day or a bad day. Because God is in our lives, we can face each day with joy and gladness knowing he's going to walk through it with us. Even an ordinary day has blessings we take for granted like the sun shining, birds singing, children laughing, and people praying. Every day is a gift from God just waiting to be unwrapped like a present to discover all its beauty.

The next time you have a bad day, remember that it's really not all bad. God made the day and he is there with you waiting to shower you with blessings if you'll only look for them.

INTERACTION OPTIONS

Medium: *Use only two helpers and have one invite you out to lunch.*

Low: *Omit helper interaction. Begin message by asking the kids if they've ever had a really good day. What makes a day good?*

This is the day the Lord has made; let us rejoice and be glad in it.

Hidden Treasure

THEME: Learning God's Word

SCRIPTURE: "I have hidden your word in my heart that I might not sin against you" (Psalm 119:11).

SUPPLIES NEEDED: A treasure chest (could be a file card box covered with construction paper or fabric and adorned with fake jewels which can be bought by the bag at a craft store.) Chocolate gold coins inside.

INTERACTION: *Someone to show you a treasure chest he found hidden behind an old loose board at his house. As helper shows the kids his treasure, someone comes and steals it from him. You tell him how sorry you are that his treasure was taken. The sad helper is seated and you continue with message.*

Leader: Hi, kids. I had an unusual thing happen to me this morning. A good friend of mine told me he found a treasure chest hidden behind an old loose board in his house. He asked if he could come this morning and show us what was inside. Come on up, (name), and show us what you found.

Helper (*comes up protectively carrying his treasure chest:*) I'll be glad to show you, but you have to promise not to damage it. No grabbing or pushing to see. Deal?

Leader: Does that sound like a deal, kids? (*Let kids respond.*) All right. Deal. (*Helper slowly opens the lid of the chest.*) Wow! That's beautiful. You must be really proud to have found such a wonderful treasure. What a surprise it must have been. Thanks for letting us see it. I feel honored to have been included in such a special treasure find.

Helper: May I share some of my treasure with the kids? It feels so good to share.

Leader: Sure you can! That would be very generous of you.

Helper (*hands a chocolate coin to each child and closes lid:*) Thank you for sticking by our deal. These are some great kids you have here. I'll be going now. I just wanted to show you my treasure. *(Just as he is leaving, someone runs through and steals the treasure from him.)*

Leader: Oh my word! Are you OK?

Helper: Yes, I'm fine. But that guy got away with my treasure. Oh, well, at least I got to share it with you.

Leader: I am so sorry. We appreciate you for taking the risk to stop by with it.

Helper: That's OK. Guess I'd better go call the police. *(Helper exits.)*

I hope (name) gets his treasure back. Wouldn't it be neat to find a hidden treasure? *(Let kids respond.)* If you found a treasure chest, what would you hope was inside? *(Let kids respond.)* There are all kinds of treasures. What things do people treasure? *(Let kids respond.)* Money, pets, family, their belongings. There are all kinds of things to treasure in this world. The only problem is that most of the things we treasure can be taken away. There's only one treasure that never changes and can never be taken from you. It's God's Word, the Bible.

Psalm 119:11 says, "I have hidden your word in my heart that I might not sin against you." Where was God's Word hidden? *(Let kids respond.)* How can you hide God's Word in your heart? *(Let kids respond.)* That's right, by memorizing verses so you'll never forget them. Then your treasure, the Bible, can never be taken from you because you've hidden it in a safe place. Why should we hide God's Word in our hearts? *(Let kids respond.)* Yes, to help us in our fight against sin. The Bible teaches us what is right and what is wrong. We can make better choices when we know what God's Word says. Or when we're discouraged, God's Word can remind us that God loves us and will see us through.

We also need to share our treasure like our friend did. How can we share God's Word? *(Let kids respond.)* By telling our friends about Jesus and inviting them to church with us. God's Word is like a hidden treasure except that it's more valuable than all the diamonds in the world, and will last forever. Treasure God's Word in your heart so you can be strong against sin, then share your treasure with your friends.

INTERACTION OPTIONS

Medium: *Someone to show you the treasure chest he found hidden behind an old loose board at his house. Omit thief.*

Low: *Pretend you found an old treasure and ask the kids if they'd like to see it.*

See No Evil

THEME: Protecting our minds from evil

SCRIPTURE: "Turn my eyes away from worthless things; preserve my life according to your word" (Psalm 119:37).

SUPPLIES NEEDED: Two pairs of sunglasses. Optional: an inexpensive pair of sunglasses to give each child.

INTERACTION: *Someone to wear one pair of sunglasses. You'll wear the other pair. Everyone in the congregation who has a pair of sunglasses will put them on.*

Leader: Good morning, kids. What a sunny day we're having. *(Helper walks up wearing sunglasses.)* What have we here?

Helper: I like to wear my shades on sunny days like today to protect my eyes.

Leader: I know what you mean. I have mine with me too. *(Put on your sunglasses.)* They sure help keep the sun out of my eyes. *(To class:)* Do any of you kids have sunglasses? *(Let kids respond.)* Why do you wear them? *(Let kids respond.)* I guess we wear them for the same reason—to keep the sun out of our eyes. The experts say sunglasses are very important for the health of our eyes. They say our eyes can be damaged by looking at the sun without protection. How many people in our congregation have sunglasses? *(Congregation gives a show of hands.)* If you have your sunglasses, would you please put them on? *(Congregation puts on their sunglasses.)* We're going to talk about protecting ourselves today, and seeing all these sunglasses may help the kids remember the lesson better.

We look like a bunch of cool dudes, don't we? What a cool congregation we have! Did you know the Bible talks about protecting our eyes? *(Let kids respond.)* But it isn't talking about using sunglasses. It's talking about protecting our eyes from things we shouldn't see—like bad movies, violence, dirty pictures, or too much TV. The Bible says these kinds of things are worthless. These things can hurt us, maybe not on the outside, but on the inside.

Do you know what a callus is? (*Let kids respond.*) A callus is a place where your skin has grown tough from being used all the time. Some people get calluses on their fingers from writing so much. The calloused skin is dead. It's hard and you can't feel anything through it. Your minds can get calloused too by seeing too many bad things. How would you feel if you saw something you shouldn't? (*Let kids respond.*) The first time you see the bad thing, whether it is violence on TV or a dirty magazine, you feel bad or embarrassed because you know you're seeing something you shouldn't. But the more often you see those things, the less they bother you. Your mind is getting calloused. It's beginning to feel less and less. It's a terrible thing to get a calloused mind because after a while you can't tell what's right and what's wrong. And when that happens, you'll find yourself in all kinds of trouble.

The author of Psalm 119:37 says, "Turn my eyes away from worthless things; preserve my life according to your word." That's a prayer we all can pray. We need to ask God's help in keeping our eyes from seeing things we shouldn't so we can live good lives. The Bible and prayer are like sunglasses. They both protect us. Just as sunglasses protect our eyes, the Bible and prayer protect our minds.

Optional closing: I brought each of you a pair of sunglasses to remind you to protect your eyes from the sun and from other harmful things. (*Pass out sunglasses.*) The sunglasses will not protect your mind though. You must ask God to remind you to turn away from things that will mess up you mind. And be sure to read your Bible to keep your mind callous-free.

INTERACTION OPTIONS

Medium: *You and helper wear your sunglasses. Omit having the congregation put on their sunglasses.*

Low: *Have your sunglasses on at the beginning of the children's message. Explain that you wear them to protect your eyes from the glaring sun.*

Turn my eyes away from worthless things.

Shield Me

THEME: God's protection

SCRIPTURE: "You are my refuge and my shield; I have put my hope in your word" (Psalm 119:114).

SUPPLIES NEEDED: One trash can lid per child. A bag full of paper wads for each adult helper. Two masking tape lines approximately ten feet apart.

INTERACTION: *One adult per child to throw paper wads at kids while they use trash can lids as shields.*

I thought it might be fun to play a game today. I've asked several people to be helpers for our game. Would our helpers please come up now?

Here's what we're going to do. Let's have all the kids line up on this line and all our helpers line up on the other line facing the kids. When I say go, our helpers will begin throwing paper wads at you, and you need to try to protect yourself with your shield. (*Hold up trash can lid. Pass out shields to kids, then give each helper a bag of paper wads.*) The helpers can't go past their line and you can't go away from yours. When I say stop, the helpers will quit throwing paper wads and you may safely lower your shields. Ready? GO! (*Let helpers throw wads for one minute or until the paper is gone, whichever comes first.*) STOP! Good work! You did a great job defending yourselves against these guys. And I think our helpers got a whole week's worth of frustration worked out! Kids, would you please stack your shields on top of each other on the floor by me? And will our helpers please gather the paper wads and put them back in the bags? Thank you for helping us. (*Helpers then return to their seats.*)

That was a crazy game, wasn't it? Good thing you had your shields for protection or you would have been goners. Where was the best place to hold your shield for protection? (*Let kids respond.*) Right in front of you. If you held it down at your side, it wouldn't do much good, would it? You had to use your shield in order for it to protect you.

Psalm 119:114 says, "You are my refuge and my shield; I have put my hope in your word." What's a refuge? *(Let kids respond.)* A refuge is a safe place. God is our refuge and our shield. We can put our trust in him and in what he says. But just like any shield, we have to lift it up for protection. We need to lift God up to be the most important thing in our lives. We need to read his Word so we'll be ready to stand against the enemy, Satan. Having a Bible sitting on a shelf won't protect us against the evil in the world. We need to read it and put the things we learn into practice so God can rule in our lives. We need to pray daily for God to help us fight the battles of each day. So raise your shield of faith and lift God up when you're tempted to do wrong. Fight the battle against sin with confidence, knowing God is on your side and will see you through.

INTERACTION OPTIONS

Medium: *Have one helper from the congregation throw paper wads at a child (or vice versa) while he tries to fend them off with his shield.*

Low: *Divide the kids into two groups. Let one group throw paper wads at the other while they defend themselves with their shields (trash can lids).*

You are my refuge and my shield; I have put my hope in your word.

Asleep on the Job

THEME: God's faithful care

SCRIPTURE: "He will not let your foot slip—he who watches over you will not slumber" (Psalm 121:3).

SUPPLIES NEEDED: Large name tags that say "Security Guard" for each guard on duty

INTERACTION: *Two or three people to play the parts of security guards. Before kids come up for the children's message, the helpers playing the security guards come up and stand watch.*

Leader: Come on up, kids. It's time for our children's message. (*Kids come up.*) As you can see, we have some security guards with us today. What are security guards for? (*Let kids respond.*) They help us feel safe.

(*Security guards begin to yawn and stretch.*) If someone were to come in here and try to hurt us, one of the security guards would walk him or her out and handle the situation so we would be safe. Security guards are hired to protect us.

(*Security guards lay down and fall asleep.*) So I thought in this day and age of rising crime it wouldn't hurt to have a few security guards around. (*You look at security guards and notice they've fallen asleep.*) Hey! What are you doing? Sleeping on the job? That doesn't make me feel very safe!

Guards (*slowly waking up:*) Huh? Oh, sorry, I guess we fell asleep. We were up pretty late last night.

Leader: Up late? But you're not doing your job if you're sleeping! You're supposed to stay awake and alert to any signs of danger so you can protect us.

Guards: Sorry! Look, we don't even know you people—why should we protect you?

Leader: Never mind. You obviously don't care about our safety. We'll protect ourselves. No sense in paying you to sleep. Go and get some rest. (*Helpers exit.*)

Can you believe those guys? The nerve of them sleeping on the job when they were supposed to be protecting us. Oh, well. We don't need them anyway. I know someone who watches over us and loves us and never sleeps on the job. He's the ultimate security guard. Can you guess who it is? (*Let kids guess.*) It's God. We can count on him to always be awake when we need him. He watches over our every step. God cares about each move we make, each decision we struggle with, every problem we face.

Psalm 121:3 says, "He will not let your foot slip—he who watches over you will not slumber." What is slumber? (*Let kids answer.*) Slumber is the same thing as sleep. That's why when you go to someone's house to sleep it's sometimes called a slumber party. It's not just a daytime party. It's when you stay overnight at your friend's house to sleep—at least a few hours! He who watches over us, God, will not sleep. Our verse says he won't even let our foot slip. We just need to follow him and ask him to guide us through our lives. It's like having a security guard in Heaven. Our heavenly security guard will never fall asleep on the job like our security guards did here this morning. You can always count on God to care enough to help you any time, day or night.

INTERACTION OPTIONS

Medium: *Use only one security guard in your message.*

Low: *Talk to the kids about security guards. Who are they? What do they do? Would you feel safe if you saw a security guard sleeping on the job?*

He will not let your foot slip—he who watches over you will not slumber.

All for One

THEME: Unity, working together

SCRIPTURE: "How good and pleasant it is when brothers live together in unity!" (Psalm 133:1).

SUPPLIES NEEDED: None

INTERACTION: *Three helpers to lead your train in different directions.*
Give an open invitation to anyone in the congregation
who would like to join the train.

Have you ever seen a train? (*Let kids respond.*) What is the front car that leads the train called? (*Let kids respond.*) That's right, it's called the engine. And wherever the engine goes, the rest of the train follows. All of the train cars arrive at their destination together. Let's be a train today. I've asked a few people to come up and help us so our train will be nice and long. (*Call your helpers up. Position them in between children so each helper has several children behind her.*) Would anyone else in the congregation like to join our train? The longer the train, the better! Hold on to the person in front of you. What sounds does a train make? (*Let kids respond.*) Sort of a chuga-chuga sound, isn't it? Let me hear you sound like a train. (*Let kids make train sound.*) And there's usually a whistle on the train that sounds like this: Whooo-oo-whooo! Who would like to be our whistle? (*Choose one or two children to be the whistle.*) The rest of us will make the train sound. Our goal is to go clear around the room and end up right back where we started. Are we ready? Let's start our train. (*Start chugging. Remind the whistle to sound occasionally, if needed. Lead train around the congregation, or a part of the sanctuary if your congregation is very large. During the journey, helpers will lead their followers off in different directions. You look back to check the progress of the train and see that parts of it are missing and going in other directions.*) Hey! What happened to our train? I thought we all were going to go in the same direction. After all, I'm the engine and you're supposed to follow me. (*Helpers reply saying they thought it looked more interesting to go these other ways.*) But look how short our train is now! We're supposed to stick together, like a team. I thought we all had the same goal in mind—to go around the congregation and arrive back up front together! (*Helpers say they never agreed to that. They wanted to do their own thing.*) Oh, OK. Let's just forget the train idea and come back up to the front and have our children's message. (*Everyone returns to usual message area.*)

Boy, that didn't work out like I planned. It seems like our train didn't work together very well. Our helpers had different ideas and plans than I did. We all went our own ways. We weren't very unified. That means we didn't think together like one train; we thought like we were each our own train. Sometimes it's good to have your own thoughts and ideas. But other times it's good to work together toward a common goal, using teamwork and unity.

Psalm 133:1 says, "How good and pleasant it is when brothers live together in unity!" As Christians, we have a goal we're trying to reach. We all want to serve God. In living our lives each day, we need to be a unified team working toward that goal. We need to encourage each other, pick each other up when we're down, and tell others about Jesus so we can all reach our goal. If we work together, we'll reach our destination better than our train did.

INTERACTION OPTIONS

Medium: *Three helpers to lead the train off in different directions. Omit invitation for congregation to join you.*

Low: *Lead your kids on the train journey without the helpers. When you return to the message, talk about what would have happened if some of them had gone off in different directions than the engine did.*

How good and pleasant it is when brothers live together in unity!

Look at Me!

THEME: Our wonderful bodies

SCRIPTURE: "I praise you because I am fearfully and wonderfully made; your works are wonderful, I know that full well" (Psalm 139:14).

SUPPLIES NEEDED: Several large bandages

INTERACTION: *A few people from the congregation wear bandages on their noses and stand with spokesman while he explains they've formed a support group for people who think their noses are too big.*

Leader: Good morning, kids. (*Helper comes toward you wearing bandage on his nose.*) (Name), what happened to your nose?

Helper: Oh, nothing. But I hate my nose because it's too big, so I decided to hide it under this bandage. As a matter of fact, I've started a new group here at church for people who think their noses are too big.

Leader: You have?

Helper: Yes. Come on up, group. (*Group with bandages on noses comes up.*) We're a support group for anyone who feels his or her nose is too large. We meet every Monday night at 7 o'clock, if you're interested in joining us.

Leader: Well, I've never thought any of you had big noses. But now that you're wearing those bandages, your noses were the first things I noticed. Kids, do you think this is a good idea? (*Let kids respond.*) I agree. Putting a bandage on your nose doesn't hide it; the bandage only draws attention to it. If you don't want people to notice your nose, just forget about it. Don't even talk about it. Then they'll see a whole person instead of some minor part of you.

Helper: You really think so? Maybe we should give that a try. (*Helper takes off his bandage and instructs the others to do the same.*) You know, I believe that is better—thanks! (*Helpers exit.*)

Is there a part of your body you don't particularly like? (*Let kids respond.*)

Sometimes people think their ears are too big, their teeth aren't white enough, or that they're too fat or too thin. Plastic surgeons make millions of dollars trying to make people look better.

Well, I've got good news for you today. You look great! In fact, you are the most beautiful people I've ever seen! You look strong and healthy. Not only that, you look happy! Look at those fabulous smiles. They're gorgeous! God made you absolutely perfect. He made you just the way he wanted you to be. God understands there may be some things about yourself you wish were different, but he has a special mission for you. And you need to be just like you are in order to do it. No one else is qualified to do your mission but you.

Now you may say "What about the kids who make fun of me?" Yeah. What about those kids? How does it make you feel when others make fun of you? (*Let kids respond.*) It hurts inside, doesn't it? God loves you and doesn't like to see you get hurt. But in this world of sinful people, you may get hurt sometimes. But God can use that hurt to make your heart soft. He knows you'll remember the pain of the teasing and you won't tease other kids in ways that hurt them because you know how bad it feels. God can use the bad things in your life to mold you into the kind of person he wants you to be.

Let's see what the Bible has to say about our bodies. In Psalm 139:14, David wrote, "I praise you because I am fearfully and wonderfully made; your works are wonderful, I know that full well." What does it mean to be fearfully made? (*Let kids respond.*) The Bible sometimes tells us to fear God. That doesn't mean to be afraid of him. It means to respect him. To be in awe of him. When we're fearfully made that means we're awesomely made. God made each of us fearfully and wonderfully. God's works are wonderful. There's no question about it. He made us so complicated that even the smartest scientists haven't been able to figure out how to create human beings that are each uniquely different.

So don't try to hide your uniqueness. You're one of God's masterpieces. Be proud of what makes you different. Stand tall and don't let teasing get to you. God made you fearfully and wonderfully. You can't get any better than that.

INTERACTION OPTIONS

Medium: *One person to wear the bandage because he thinks his nose is too big.*

Low: *Wear a bandage to hide your nose. Explain to the kids why you're wearing it. Ask them if they think people will notice your nose less with it on.*